And Who Loves Me?

Hortense Ullrich

And Who Loves Me?

Aus dem Deutschen
von David Fermer

Thienemann

Friday 5th January

Alone at last!

Well, alone with Sven at least. That was **a big deal**.

You see, Lucilla's usually around. She's my best friend and is **convinced** that it's her job to make sure Sven and I have a really romantic afternoon. That's why she **constantly** organizes activities for us.

She always gives me a **lecture**. "You two need more romance in your relationship," she says. "It's really important!"

I can only say she's right. Perhaps things would be a little bit more romantic if Lucilla wasn't always with us. She **accompanies** us wherever we go, giving instructions and checking we're doing everything right.

When Sven kissed me **recently** on the street, she threw herself between us and shouted, "Not here!"

"Why not?" I asked **with a start**.

---

a big deal – eine große Sache; convinced – überzeugt;
constantly – dauernd; lecture – Vortrag;
to accompany – begleiten; recently – neulich;
with a start – erschrocken

Lucilla pointed to the **building site** next to us.

"Not next to a building site! That's completely unromantic!"

Sven **banged** his head with his hand. "I'm such a **dork**! How could I let that happen?"

Lucilla nodded full of **forgiveness**.

Sven cast a **reproachful** glance at me. "Jojo! How could you let this happen?!"

"What are you talking about?" I said, **outraged**. "I didn't see the building site either."

Sven rolled his eyes. Then I realized he'd meant it ironically. "Sorry," I apologized **sheepishly** to Sven. "I'm a bit **under the weather** at the moment."

That was true. **For some reason** I'd lost my sense of humour recently. Lucilla's constant **presence** was getting more and more on my nerves.

It was about time I went out with Sven alone again. Without Lucilla.

And today it's finally going to happen. I'm going to the cinema later. With Sven. And without Lucilla. I've made it. Hurray!

I'm quite **proud of** myself really.

I had to tell Sven **without delay**. I gave him a call

---

building site – Baustelle; to bang – schlagen; dork – Dummkopf; forgiveness – Vergebung; reproachful – vorwurfsvoll; outraged – empört; sheepish – kleinlaut; to be under the weather – angeschlagen sein; for some reason – irgendwie; presence – Anwesenheit; to be proud of – stolz sein auf; without delay – ohne Verzögerung, sofort and said **straightaway**, "Okey-dokey! The coast is clear."

"Hello, Josefine," said Sven's mum somewhat **reticently**. "I'm fine, thank you. And how are you?"

It was really **embarrassing**. "I'm sorry I didn't **introduce myself** properly, it's just ... "

"Don't worry about it. I recognized you straightaway ... " and I thought she was going to finish her sentence with "from your bad telephone **manners**".

I wanted to **make up for** it and said in my very best manners, "May I speak to your son, please?"

But Sven's mum was already on her way. Bad manners, I would say.

Shortly afterwards Sven picked up the phone. He sounded in a good **mood**, though my enthusiasm had been somewhat **dampened**.

"Everything's **hunky-dory**," I told him **feebly**.

"What are you talking about?"

"Code word: Lucilla!"

"What about her? Have you joined the **Secret Service**? Why are you talking so cryptically?"

Cryptically? Another word I have to look up in the dictionary.

---

straightaway – sofort; reticent – zurückhaltend;
embarrassing – peinlich;
to introduce (oneself) – (sich) vorstellen;
manners – Manieren;
to make up for sth – etwas wiedergutmachen;
mood – Stimmung, Laune; to dampen – dämpfen;
hunky-dory – paletti; feeble – *hier:* lahm;
Secret Service – Geheimdienst

"Man, Sven, I **got rid of** Lucilla. We're alone this evening!"

"I can't believe it! I never thought that would ever happen again. How did you **pull** that **off**?"

"Well," I said proudly, "I'm a master of tactics."

To be **honest**, it didn't have much to do with tactics. The truth was, Lucilla didn't have any time because her grandmother was coming to visit. But Sven didn't have to know that.

"Respect! Perhaps something will come of you one day," said Sven, **impressed**. "So, what are we going to do with our afternoon **off** then? Look for some building sites?"

"Cinema!" I said **decisively**.

Lucilla hadn't allowed me and Sven to go to the cinema for weeks because she **claimed** it was completely unromantic. All you do is sit next to each other for two hours without talking and without looking each other **lovingly** in the eyes.

She kept trying to **persuade** us to take moonlit walks. Great idea for someone like me who always has to be home at 8pm. The most I could make would be an early **sunset** in winter. And that's not exactly romantic when you live in a city where the

---

to get rid of sth – etwas loswerden;
to pull sth off – etwas schaffen; honest – ehrlich;
impressed – beeindruckt; off – frei;
decisive – entschlossen; to claim – behaupten;
loving – liebevoll; to persuade – überreden;
sunset – Sonnenuntergang

grey winter days move **seamlessly** into the neon lights of the late afternoon.

But today Sven and I are going to have a romantic movie **matinée**. And before that we're going to go to **every single** building site in town and – that's right – kiss! So there!

Saturday 6th January

Well, great! **So much for** a romantic movie matinée with Sven.

It all started off pretty strangely. I should have known then that it wasn't my day.

Just as we sat down, I dropped my popcorn and **spilt** Sven's Coke. One quick movement of the hand and there it was. All over the place. You can't beat me when it comes to spilling things. All I wanted to do was check the time on my watch. Sven had asked me what the time was. It was only when I was already **twisting** my **wrist** that I realized this was the hand holding the popcorn. It was too late to stop the movement, so I hectically tried to catch the **tub** with the other hand. That's when I spilt Sven's Coke.

---

seamless – nahtlos; matinée – Frühvorstellung;
every single – jeder einzelne;
so much for – von wegen; to spill – verschütten;
to twist – drehen; wrist – Handgelenk; tub – Becher

Sven generously ignored the chaos. He repeated his question **as cool as a cucumber**: "So, what time is it?"

"Time for another tub of popcorn and a fresh Coke," I replied, standing up and leaving the **auditorium**.

What's said is done, no turning back.

After having bought a new Coke and another tub of popcorn, I made my way back to Sven. These modern multiplexes which show at least five films at the same time are not really as great as they sound. I know that now.

When I came back into the auditorium, the advertising had already started. The lights were out.

But that **didn't matter**. I knew where Sven was sitting.

Besides, I'd always recognize him. Even from behind in the dark. That's love for you.

I **headed towards** him, sat down in the seat next to him, gave him his Coke and a kiss.

"Wow!" said the guy who I'd just kissed. "This is so cool!"

I dropped my popcorn with a start and jumped to my feet.

It wasn't Sven. I'd just kissed a complete **stranger**!

---

as cool as a cucumber – mit einem kühlen Kopf;
auditorium – Saal; it doesn't matter – es macht nichts;
besides – außerdem;
to head towards sth/sb – auf etwas/jmdn. zusteuern;
stranger – Fremde/Fremder

It was unbelievable. It was the most embarrassing thing I've ever done.

I stared into the guy's face and things went from bad to worse. He wasn't a complete stranger. It was Marc. **Of all people**!

Marc is really good-looking, but he has the **brains** of soup **can** and has been Carla's boyfriend for as long as I can remember.

I was just thinking how lucky it was that Carla hadn't **witnessed** this terrible moment when a girl sitting on the other side of Marc **leant forward** and said, "This is a cinema, not a **dating agency**." It was Carla. As she recognized me, her eyes almost popped out of her head. "Of course! I could have guessed! Josefine Sonntag. Who else would **dare** do a thing like that?"

"I'm sorry," I stuttered, grabbed the tub of popcorn, which was now empty again, and ran off.

In the safety of the darkness I **stumbled** back to sort my head out. It was mega-embarrassing. The whole thing was bad enough, but to have kissed Carla's boyfriend of all people!

Carla is known for being a seriously cool **chick**. Classmates who become **victims** of her **bitchy, cut-**

---

of all people – ausgerechnet; brains – Intelligenz;
can – Dose; to witness – sehen; to lean forward – sich vorbeugen; dating agency – Kontaktbörse;
to dare – es wagen; to stumble – stolpern;
chick – *hier:* Mädchen; victim – Opfer;
bitchy, cutting comments – gemeine, spitze Bemerkungen

ting comments usually had to be sent to the school's sick room for **treatment**.

And then there was the thing with the rucksack and Carla's hair. She wasn't going to **forgive** me too soon for that – even though it had been an accident. Unfortunately, a really embarrassing one though.

Two days ago I saw Carla leaning over a rucksack, **rummaging around** inside.

"Isn't that *your* rucksack?" Lucilla said to me.

Hey! She was right. That was my rucksack! What was Carla doing **sniffing around** in *my* rucksack?

I went over to her and tried to pull the rucksack out of her hands, but she wouldn't **let go**. I quickly did up the **zip** so that at least she couldn't rummage around in it any more. Unfortunately, Carla's hair **got caught** in the zip. So much so that she couldn't get out of it.

Cursing me, Carla went to the school doctor with the rucksack on her ear. He **made short work** of it and just cut off the hair that had got caught up in the zip. It didn't exactly look like a cool haircut, more like Carla had fallen down the stairs. Carla was so angry she almost killed me.

---

treatment – Behandlung; to forgive – verzeihen;
to rummage around – herumwühlen;
to sniff around – rumschnüffeln; to let go – loslassen;
zip – Reißverschluss; to get caught – eingeklemmt werden;
to curse – fluchen, *hier:* beschimpfen;
to make short work – kurzen Prozess machen

What's more, the rucksack wasn't even mine. It was Carla's. Rucksacks all look the same these days. I mean, how was I to know …? Anyway, it didn't exactly put me on Carla's Top Ten Best Friends list.

And now this! What a **botch-up**.

Why did this have to happen to me?!

After thinking about it for a second, I decided it was all Sven's **fault**. He'd probably changed seats!

Damn it, why did Sven do that? If it was meant to be a joke, I couldn't see what was funny about it.

Then the film started.

Another reason **to get worked up**: It wasn't the film Sven and I had come to see. Sven is a real **airhead**.

And where was the guy sitting anyway?!

"Sven," I called as quietly as possible.

Nothing.

"Sven!" I called a bit louder.

"Sve-en!"

The **usher** came up to me, told me to stop shouting and **reminded** me where I was.

I told the usher to stop telling me what to do and reminded him that it was the cinema's fault because they were showing the wrong film.

He wanted to see my ticket. That's typical. Whenever these kind of people don't know what to do, they ask to see your ticket or some other document.

---

what's more – außerdem; botch-up – Murks; fault – Schuld; to get worked up – sich aufregen; airhead – Dussel; usher – Platzanweiser; to remind sb – jmdn. erinnern

I **haughtily** gave him my ticket. He **shone his torch** at it and said I was a real **dopey** idiot. I was in the wrong cinema.

I **had a go at** him back: if he'd been at the entrance doing his job **instead of** hiding in the auditorium, then this wouldn't have happened at all. And then I wouldn't have kissed Marc!

He didn't really know what to make of my last comment.

I went out again and it took me a while to **calm** myself **down** and find the way to the right cinema.

I sat down next to Sven, feeling **exhausted,** and was just about to tell him about what had happened to me when he said, "Where's my Coke?"

"What would you say if I told you I gave it to somebody else? A boy. And not just that. I gave him a kiss, too."

"Doesn't sound good to me," said Sven. "Haven't you got a better **excuse**?"

"There was no Coke left," I **suggested**.

"No popcorn either?" asked Sven, looking into my empty tub.

"That's right!"

---

haughty – hochmütig;
to shine a torch – etwas mit einer Taschenlampe anstrahlen;
dopey – benebelt; to have a go at sb – jmdn. anmeckern;
instead of – statt; to calm down – sich beruhigen;
exhausted – erschöpft; excuse – Ausrede;
to suggest – vorschlagen

"Then I'll take the first **explanation**," decided Sven. "It's more **plausible**."

"It was an accident," I tried to explain.

Sven grinned and took me in his arms. "I know."

"Sshhh!" **hissed** the people behind us.

I turned around. "I'm terribly sorry, but I just had ..."

"Quiet!" shouted somebody.

Okay, okay. If you don't want to hear my story ...

Two minutes later someone tapped me on the shoulder and said, "**Budge up**!"

It was Lucilla. She **clambered** over the back of the chair and sat down between me and Sven.

Sven **stifled a laugh**.

I looked at Lucilla horrified. "How did you know ...? Where did you ...?" I stuttered.

"Oh, come on, I could hardly help **overhearing** you. I'm sorry I'm late. Our telephone's broken – in case you tried to call ..."

"We didn't even try to c...," I started to say, but then I just said miserably, "Your grandma wanted to come."

Sven looked at me and said quietly, "Great plan, Jojo, inviting her grandma."

---

explanation – Erklärung; plausible – glaubwürdig;
to hiss – zischen; to budge up – aufrücken;
to clamber – klettern;
to stifle a laugh – sich das Lachen verbeißen;
to overhear – etwas zufällig mithören

I felt like I'd been **caught red-handed**. I sank into my seat and kept my mouth shut.

"My grandma didn't come. That's why I've got time for you both now."

"I see. And how did you know we were here?" I asked.

"Your mum told me. **Otherwise** I would never have found you."

Great! Thanks a lot, Mum! We'll have to have a serious talk about this when I get home.

After a while Lucilla **nudged** me. "Why did you decide to go to the cinema, Jojo?!" she asked in a whisper. "I've told you so often: the cinema is really unromantic!"

I sighed and tried to hold hands with Sven behind Lucilla's back.

When the film came to an end, my arm was **dead** and despite my **attempts** at gymnastics, I couldn't get any life back into it.

On the way out I was still shaking my arm like crazy when suddenly Lucilla started to wave her arms around as well. "Hi, Carla! We're here!" she cried.

That was just what I needed!

Lucilla is **in awe of** Carla because Carla is so cool. The truth is: Carla's coolness is nothing more than being **rude** to people the whole time.

---

to catch sb red-handed – jmdn. auf frischer Tat ertappen;
otherwise – sonst; to nudge – stupsen;
dead – *hier:* eingeschlafen; attempt – Versuch;
to be in awe of sb – jmdn. bewundern;
rude – unverschämt

Carla headed straight towards us. She was **up for a fight**. "How nice! Were you in a kiddies' film again?" Before I could say anything, she added, "Don't worry, when I was ten, I never got into **grown-up** films either."

"But we're 13!" Lucilla clarified **needlessly**. After all, we're in the same class.

I decided to keep my mouth shut. Since the embarrassing **incident** with Carla's hair I was trying not to be so **cheeky** to her, and I usually **swallowed** her cutting comments without saying anything. That's the way I wanted to keep it. At least until her hair has grown back.

Marc came up to me looking friendly and said, "Thanks for the Coke. You disappeared so quickly, I couldn't …" But he didn't finish his sentence. Carla made sure of that.

Carla just leant towards me and hissed, "Go to the **lonely hearts ball** if you don't fancy your boyfriend any more. Or take a look on the Internet. But keep your hands off Marc! Understand?"

"It was an accident!"

"Then get yourself a pair of glasses, you **mole**," she hissed at me and **stomped off**, pulling Marc

---

to be up for a fight – in Kampfstimmung sein;
grown-up – Erwachsene/Erwachsener;
needlessly – unnötigerweise; incident – Vorfall;
cheeky – frech; to swallow – schlucken;
lonely hearts ball – Ball der einsamen Herzen;
mole – Maulwurf; to stomp off – davonstapfen

along with her. He looked like he was **getting a real earful**.

"You gave my Coke to *Marc*?" said Sven.

"What do you understand under the **term** 'my' Coke?" I asked him.

He didn't find that funny. "**I'd rather** you kissed complete strangers than guys I know," he said, giving me a **weary** look.

"Me, too! Believe me!"

Lucilla stared at me with wide-open eyes and **squealed** shrilly, "You kissed Marc?"

"An accident! It was an accident!"

Lucilla looked at me in amazement. "How can you accidentally kiss someone?"

I **shrugged**. Only I was **capable** of doing things like that.

"How did it happen?" asked Lucilla. "And what did Carla say?"

I **waved my hand dismissively**. "You don't want to know."

"Oh yes, I do," nodded Lucilla, "otherwise I wouldn't have asked."

Sven saved me. He put his arms around us. "I'm in the mood for a bit of romance," he said softly. "Any ideas, Lucilla?"

---

to get an earful – etwas zu hören bekommen;
term – Ausdruck; I'd rather – mir wäre es lieber;
weary – müde; to squeal – quietschen;
to shrug – die Achseln zucken; capable – fähig;
to wave one's hand dismissively – abwinken

Lucilla gave a big smile. I rolled my eyes. Sven was being **outrageous**. He knew perfectly well that all that got on my nerves.

"Actually, I wanted to go home," I said **snottily**.

Lucilla laughed. "Oh, come on! What about a nice romantic dinner?"

"I'm not hungry," I replied.

Sven never misses a chance. "That'll be because of all the popcorn you ate," he said.

I kept quiet, feeling **offended**.

"I've got a **coupon** for *Bratwurst* at the Balkan Grill!" cried Lucilla delighted, waving a piece of paper in the air. Sven rolled his eyes in **blissful anticipation**. "Oh great! Fried sausage!"

"You can't get more romantic than that!" I said **grumpily**, **aiming** my comment **at** Sven, but only offending Lucilla in the end.

"I only mean well," she said miserably.

I immediately apologized. "I'm sorry, Lucilla. It really is very nice of you."

A short time later we were standing in front of the Balkan Grill with Lucilla, eating a romantic *Bratwurst* in the freezing cold and listening to Lucilla giving us a lecture on "the nature of romance" and how to recognize the first signs of crisis in a relationship.

---

outrageous – unmöglich; snotty – patzig;
offended – beleidigt; coupon – Gutschein;
blissful anticipation – glückselige Vorfreude;
grumpy – mürrisch; to aim at – (ab)zielen auf

Monday 8th January

The first thing Lucilla did at school this morning was give me a lecture.

"You haven't been very nice to Sven recently."

"That's not true!"

"Oh yes, it is. I've seen it myself. You're nearly always in a bad mood when the three of us are together."

I **kept quiet**. I can hardly tell Lucilla it's her fault and has nothing to do with Sven.

"You're going to have to do something if you want to keep him," said Lucilla.

For some reason the conversation with Lucilla made me feel **uneasy**. What if she was right? It's true, I really am always in a bad mood when Lucilla's around. Perhaps my bad mood is beginning to get on Sven's nerves.

On top of that Sven is starting to **annoy** me because he doesn't seem to **be bothered** by Lucilla being around.

I mean, if he really loves me, then surely he wants to be alone with me. He should say things like "Stop bringing your friend along, will you?!" and "I just want to be alone with you!"

But what does he do? Nothing! He's in a good mood and has no problem with Lucilla. **In fact**,

---

to keep quiet – schweigen; uneasy – besorgt; on top of that – darüber hinaus; to annoy – ärgern; to be bothered – sich gestört fühlen; in fact – genau genommen

Lucilla and Sven seem to have more fun with each other than I do. I just sit there in a bad mood.

Well, Lucilla may **possibly** be right and I might be in the middle of **ruining** my perfect relationship with Sven.

Tuesday 9th January

This afternoon there was a **knock** on my bedroom door. Sven **poked** his head into my room and said in a **hushed** voice, “Is the coast clear?”

“My mum’s here.”

“I know. She let me in. I’m talking about Lucilla.”

“She’s not here.”

“Good,” said Sven. He came into my room and started **pacing** up and down nervously.

“We have to talk,” was Sven’s start to our conversation.

I immediately had this **sickening** feeling in my stomach. I’d heard about conversations like this before. It was the beginning of the end. Lucilla had been right. It was over. Sven was about **to break it to me gently**.

---

possibly – womöglich;
to ruin – zerstören; knock – Klopfen;
to poke – stecken, *hier:* strecken; hushed – flüsternd;
to pace – schnell gehen; sickening – ekelhaft;
to break sth to sb gently – jmdm. etwas schonend beibringen

"What are you trying to say?" I asked in a **squeaky** voice.

"It can't go on like this," said Sven, deadly serious.

The panic started to rise up in me. Sven was angry with me. I couldn't blame him either. My endless **state** of chaos and my bad moods must have really been getting on his nerves. And now it had come to this. He didn't want to have anything to do with me any more. But I wasn't going to give up without a fight.

"Okay, if you want to be like that, then let's just forget it," I said feeling offended and turning my back to Sven to stare at the wall. So much for my **fighting spirit**!

"What are you talking about?" asked Sven in surprise.

"Oh … I don't know. What are you talking about?" I asked, suddenly feeling unsure of myself and turning back to him.

"I'm talking about Lucilla, of course!"

I threw my arms around his neck and kissed him. Thank God for that! This was all about Lucilla.

"Wow!" said Sven with a grin. "Are you always going to do that when I say Lucilla's name?"

I was so happy all I could do was **coo**.

"No, seriously now," Sven went back to the **topic**

---

squeaky – piepsig; state – Zustand;
fighting spirit – Kampfgeist;
to coo – gurren; topic – Thema

and pushed me away a little. "You're always in such a bad mood when Lucilla's around, it's **unbearable**."

I shrugged my shoulders.

"Do you always have to bring her with you?"

"It has nothing to do with me. She comes on her own," I explained. "It gets on my nerves," I added with a **guilty conscience**.

"You see, that's what I mean. I don't care if she comes along or not, but if it always puts you in a bad mood, then, of course, I do care. So either **get a grip on yourself** and be normal when she's around, or tell her she shouldn't come along all the time."

"I can't do that."

"What? You can't be normal? It's just as I feared …"

"No, I can't tell her not to come along. That's the classic situation."

"Sorry?"

"You know, as soon as a girl gets a boyfriend she forgets about her friends. I don't want to be like that!"

"I'm not saying your should forget about her! You can still meet up – just without me. And we can meet up without Lucilla."

I pulled an unhappy face.

"If she's your friend, she'll understand."

---

unbearable – unerträglich;
guilty conscience – schlechtes Gewissen;
to get a grip on oneself – sich einkriegen

I gave Sven a long look. It sounded so easy, the way he said it. He was right: I just had to talk to Lucilla. I'd explain that there were times when I wanted to be alone with Sven. It wouldn't be such a big deal. Easy.

"Okay," I said.

"Okay?"

I shrugged my shoulders. "Yeah, okay, I'll tell her."

Sven was **astonished**. "That went well. I was expecting a bit more **resistance**. I prepared myself for this conversation – I've got loads of arguments **and stuff** – and now you just say 'okay'?!"

"That's right," I said with a big smile, "if there's nothing else that **bothers** you."

Sven nodded, sat down at my desk and started to look through my school books.

Just to be on the safe side I asked again. "There isn't anything else, is there?"

"What else should there be?" he asked and took out my English exercise book. He'd **promised** to help me with my English, because we're going to have a test.

"Well, you know ..." I **hummed and hawed** a bit, feeling embarrassed. "I mean, well, you do like me, don't you?"

---

astonished – erstaunt; resistance – Widerstand;
... and stuff – ... und so; to bother – stören;
to promise – versprechen;
to hum and haw – herumdrucksen

Sven laughed. "Liking you is a must. No one would do it **voluntarily**."

That wasn't what I wanted to hear from him. Sven just doesn't know how to give someone a compliment. All I wanted to hear was that he was madly in love with me. "I think you should **rephrase** that."

Sven nodded. "How about: I lost a **bet**. That's why I have to spend all my free time with you?"

I looked at him **crossly**.

"Better?" asked Sven **smugly**.

"Worse!" I said, **scowling**.

Sven grinned.

I stamped my foot crossly. "Sven, stop being so **mean**! You know perfectly well what I want to hear!"

He stood up, took me in his arms and kissed me.

Okay, it's a good start. Now for the heartfelt **declaration of love**.

"You're the only girl I know who doesn't **slap** me when I kiss her. How was that?"

I hit him on the arm. "Forget it. You're completely unromantic! Lucilla's right. Our relationship needs more romance."

Sven grinned. "While we're back on the topic … Are you sure you can pull it off with Lucilla?"

---

voluntary – freiwillig; to rephrase – neu formulieren;
bet – Wette; cross – verärgert; smug – blasiert;
to scowl – finster blicken; mean – gemein;
declaration of love – Liebeserklärung;
to slap – eine Ohrfeige geben

"Yeah, of course, it's **a piece of cake**."

Sven seemed sceptical. Then he looked at his watch. "Not bad at all. Almost a whole 30 minutes without Lucilla. I thought she was going to be here."

I nodded. "She's coming at 4 o'clock. She wants to **revise** with us."

"Oh, great! That means in at least ten minutes you're going to be in a bad mood again."

"No, I won't!" I **grumbled**.

"You are already!"

Sven was right. I actually was in a bad mood already. And things didn't get any better when Lucilla turned up.

Nor did we revise together. Lucilla had brought a few magazine **cuttings** with her about silly situations on the theme of romance. Sven tried to **incorporate** them into our revision and asked Lucilla to translate them into English, but Lucilla **refused**.

"That definitely won't be in the test," she said naïvely.

That's when Sven gave up and went home. He squeezed the article on romance into my hand and said, "And by tomorrow you have to learn this **off by heart**. I'll be testing you."

Lucilla **giggled**. I just rolled my eyes.

---

a piece of cake – ein Kinderspiel; to revise – lernen;
to grumble – schimpfen; cutting – Ausschnitt;
to incorporate – einbeziehen; to refuse – sich weigern;
off by heart – auswendig; to giggle – kichern

In the corridor Sven **tripped over** my little sister, Flippi. She was building a strange construction on the floor.

Sven made a **daring** jump to **avoid** landing on Flippi and her chaos.

I rushed out of my room and grabbed Flippi by the arm. "You can't just dump your rubbish in front of my door!"

Flippi **bit** my hand and I let her go. She **stuck her tongue out** at me and sat back down on the floor.

"Hello, Flippi!" said Sven **cheerfully**.

The fact that he thinks Flippi is cute and funny often makes me wonder about his **sanity**. Flippi is a pest. She thinks that it's the job of a little sister to make my life difficult and **drive** me towards **madness**. I've been trying to persuade Mum to give Flippi up for adoption for years, but she seems to **be attached to** her.

Sven pointed at the **mess** on the floor. "What is that?"

"A fitness **trail** for my snails. We have to work on their fitness. They don't have any **stamina**."

Flippi is a **self-proclaimed** snail **breeder** and is

---

to trip over sth – über etwas stolpern; daring – wagemutig; to avoid – vermeiden; to bite – beißen; to stick one's tongue out – seine Zunge rausstrecken; cheerful – fröhlich; sanity – Verstand; to drive – *hier:* treiben; madness – Wahnsinn; to be attached to sb – an jmdm. hängen; mess – Durcheinander; trail – Pfad; stamina – Ausdauer; self-proclaimed – selbst ernannt; breeder – Züchter currently developing a new breed: **martial-arts-snails**.

"What about sumo wrestling?" Sven continued the conversation.

Flippi broke into a big smile. She loves talking to people about her snails. "I've already thought about that. I can't get them fat enough."

"If you need a **referee**, just let me know," said Sven. Then he took me in his arms, gave me a kiss on the nose and said, "Jojo can help out as a nurse if one of the snails gets hurt."

"Urgh," squealed Flippi and I both at the same time – me because I didn't like the idea of **bandaging injured** snails, Flippi because Sven kissed me.

Flippi jumped up, made a cross with two fingers and held them up to **ward** us **off**. "Keep your distance! Don't come any closer! Your lovey-dovey **waffle** might be **contagious**."

"Puberty is contagious," explained Sven. "Not love."

"Urgh!" screamed Flippi und backed off.

I caught sight of Flippi's snail-trail and **turned pale**. "Hey, wait a minute, you **wally**!" I shouted. "Where's my brand new rucksack?"

The question was completely irrelevant because

---

martial arts – Kampfsport; referee – Ringrichter;
to bandage – verbinden; injured – verletzt;
to ward off – abwehren; waffle – Gesülze;
contagious – ansteckend; to turn pale – blass werden;
wally – Volltrottel

I was staring straight at it: it was lying on the floor, open. Flippi had obviously chosen it to be the snails' **HQ**. Inside were at least seven snails.

"Mu-um!" I screamed as loud as I could.

When my mum finally turned up, Sven turned to me and said, "So, now that a sensible adult has arrived at the **scene of the crime**, I'm going." Then he looked at my mum and, with a glance at me and Flippi, said, "Good luck."

My mum rolled her eyes and nodded.

I don't like the way my mum and Sven **get on** all the time. It's really embarrassing. Mums shouldn't always have the same opinion as their daughters' boyfriends. It's completely uncool.

Wednesday 10th January

"I brought you guys some tickets for the concert," said Lucilla first thing in the morning at school.

Lucilla always gets hold of the best tickets because her dad works at the **council's** press office.

"Hey, cool! Who's playing?" I asked delighted.

"The philharmonic!"

Never heard of them. "Are they some new band? Are they in the charts?"

HQ = headquarters – Hauptquartier;
scene of the crime – Tatort; to get on – sich verstehen;
council – Stadtrat

Lucilla gave me a **baffled** look. “I don’t think so. They’re playing Mozart.”

“Mozart?” I squeaked. “Why Mozart?” Then it **dawned on** me. “Don’t tell me they play classical music!”

Lucilla shrugged her shoulders. “Okay, then I won’t tell you. But you’re right.”

“Lucilla!” I said reproachfully. “What makes you come up with the idea of getting tickets for a classical concert?”

“First of all they’re free and secondly …” she said, sounding **strict**, “classical music is totally *romantic*!”

Of course! Lucilla was trying to **sort out** the romance in my life with Sven. All of a sudden, I remembered: I really had to talk to Lucilla about the situation soon.

But I didn’t **stand a chance**.

Lucilla was really hot on the idea. “First of all we go to the ice-cream shop. There you order the ‘Romance **Tub**’.”

I looked at her in amazement.

“The extra-large tub for two people,” explained Lucilla. “Then you can eat together.”

“The whole tub?” I asked thoughtlessly.

“Well, if you don’t finish it, it’s not the end of the world. After all, I’ll be there!”

---

baffled – verwirrt; to dawn on sb – jmdm. dämmert etwas;
strict – streng; to sort out – regeln;
to not stand a chance – keine Chance haben;
tub – *hier:* Eisbecher

Aha. So that was the answer to that problem.

"It'll be totally romantic!" squealed Lucilla, **over the moon**.

I gave a **crooked** smile. "That's true. Romantic. Exactly."

Lucilla smiled sweetly and put her arm around my shoulder. "Did you forget about it again? Oh, Jojo, how can things **work out** between you and Sven if you don't bring a bit of romance into your relationship?"

I **sighed**. That was my **cue**. It was the perfect moment to tell her, "Listen, Lucilla, now that you mention romance ... I've been thinking about that a lot recently and I've got the feeling the whole romance thing would work out better if you just left me and Sven on our own sometimes."

Hey, it can't be that difficult to say. I just had to do it. Now. Yes, I would be open and honest about it. What could possibly go wrong?

Just **pluck up your courage**. "Er, Lucilla ... I really have to talk to you about something."

Lucilla nodded **expectantly**.

I just didn't know how to begin.

Lucilla suddenly broke into a smile. "Don't say anything. I know what this is about!"

---

over the moon – überglücklich; crooked – schräg;
to work out – klappen; to sigh – seufzen;
cue – Stichwort;
to pluck up one's courage – allen Mut zusammennehmen;
expectant – erwartungsvoll

I was really **relieved**. It was much easier than I'd thought.

"The answer is: yes!" continued Lucilla.

I gave her a smile full of **gratitude**. "You're a really good friend. Thanks for being so understanding."

"Oh, don't mention it," said Lucilla **humbly**, waving her hand dismissively. "I don't mind **lending** it to you at all."

"Thanks," I said.

Hold on a moment. What did she want to lend me?

I must have spoken my thoughts out loud because, all of a sudden, Lucilla said, "My new jumper! The one you think is so great. The one you wanted to have, but your mum said it was too expensive!"

"Oh," I said with **a sinking feeling**.

"Don't worry about it. I can wear something else. I don't need to **impress** Sven."

Now I felt really awful. Lucilla was being sooo sweet and kind to me and all I wanted to do was get rid of her.

"When is the concert?" I asked unenthusiastically.

"This afternoon. I can come around to your

---

relieved – erleichtert; gratitude – Dankbarkeit;
humble – bescheiden; to lend – leihen;
a sinking feeling – ein flaues Gefühl;
to impress – beeindrucken

place a bit earlier. Then we can look for something which goes with the jumper."

I nodded **despondently** and **submitted myself to my fate**.

And that's how the three of us ended up eating from one "Romance Tub" and then listening to Mozart.

Sven didn't say a word about the fact Lucilla was with us. He and Lucilla **talked shop** about Mozart in particular and classical music in general.

I sat there in silence because I had no idea about either **matters** and couldn't **join in** the conversation. To be fair, Lucilla didn't **have a clue** either, but that didn't stop her from talking like she was an expert.

I got more and more annoyed – particularly because it didn't seem to bother Sven that Lucilla was with us again.

"Well, this is just a great afternoon!" I **complained** quietly to Sven.

"Self-made **suffering**," whispered Sven lovingly into my ear. That didn't exactly help.

---

despondent – niedergeschlagen;
to submit oneself to one's fate – sich seinem Schicksal fügen; to talk shop – fachsimpeln;
matter – Sache, Angelegenheit; to join in – mitmachen;
to have a clue – eine Ahnung haben;
to complain – beschweren; suffering – Leiden

Unfortunately, something incredibly embarrassing happened to me during the concert.

I was bored and feeling **increasingly** miserable. I started rummaging around inside my rucksack, looking for a piece of chocolate. Chocolate is supposed to make you happy. I found **various** little **items** in my rucksack most of which I was unable to identify. So I fished them all out. I hoped to find something chocolately amongst the things. As I took each item out of my bag, I felt it in my hand, trying to find out if it was chocolate or not.

After feeling one object, I screamed and threw all the items into the air in absolute horror. They flew onto the people sitting around me. Everybody turned to me and gave me an angry look.

"What's going on?" whispered Sven. "Is there something wrong with the way the first violinist is playing? He was a bit **shaky** at one point, but it wasn't that bad."

My whole body was still **trembling** with **repulsion**. "I think I just found Benno in my rucksack. Or it could have been Hasso. I can't tell the difference."

Sven looked at me somewhat **anxiously** and asked, "What are you talking about?"

"The snails! Flippi's martial-arts-snails. She left them in my rucksack. I think one of them was inside!"

---

increasing – zunehmend; various – verschieden;
item – Gegenstand; shaky – unsicher; to tremble – zittern;
repulsion – Abscheu; anxious – besorgt

Sven tried to calm me down. “Don’t let it bother you, we’ll look for her later!”

“That’s not the problem! I don’t care about the stupid snail! Flippi will pay for this!”

After all the people had left, we **searched** between the chairs for the things I’d thrown into the air. We found a lot of things, but **not one single** snail.

All of a sudden, Sven **picked** something **up** and said, “Hold out your hand and close your eyes, Jojo.”

I really have no idea why I did what he said, but when I felt Sven put something into my hand, the concert scene was repeated all over again: I screamed and **hurled** the thing across the concert hall.

Sven caught it **skilfully** and laughed.

“How could you put a snail into my hand?” I shouted at him.

He was still laughing as he slowly opened his hand.

I was really embarrassed. The thing I’d thought was a snail was in fact no more than a big, fat, old **wine gum**.

Sven was still grinning. “If I found a wine gum this size in my rucksack, then I would scream as well!”

---

to search – suchen;
not one single – kein einziger; to pick up – aufheben;
to hurl – schleudern; skilful – geschickt;
wine gum – Weingummi

Lucilla took a look into the **palm** of Sven's hand. "Is it still **edible**?" she asked.

"Man, you two are so silly!" I grumbled and stormed off.

Thursday 11th January

I decided that the embarrassing situation at the concert was all Flippi's fault and I planned to **give her a** good **telling-off** when I saw her. After all, if she hadn't started the Snail Olympics in my rucksack, then I would never have thought that the big, fat, old wine gum could possibly have been a snail.

Flippi was sitting in the kitchen and my mum was making her a hot chocolate. That's not a good sign. My mum only ever makes Flippi a hot chocolate when Flippi is worried about something. When my mum gets the feeling that something is not right with me, she always brings me a cup of tea.

I thought: before I **steamroller** her, maybe I should find out what's bothering her.

But before I'd even asked, my mum turned to me with a look of **grief** and said, "Something terrible has happened, Jojo. Fred has **disappeared**!"

---

palm – Handfläche; edible – essbar;
to give sb a telling-off – jmdm. die Leviten lesen;
to steamroller – niederbügeln; grief – tiefe Trauer;
to disappear – verschwinden

"Fred?"

"Fred, the leader of the martial-arts-snails," said Mum with a **meaningful** nod towards Flippi.

I did my best to pull a face full of **remorse**. Then I shot up in surprise. Oh my God! So it was Fred who I threw across the concert hall yesterday. And the **poor devil** was still lying there.

"I didn't do it **on purpose**," I said, **leaping to my defence** immediately. "How was I meant to know he was in my rucksack? I thought it was a wine gum." Then I bit my lip. That was really stupid of me. "Hold on – I was only joking! It really was a wine gum. Lucilla ate it."

"What are you talking about, Jojo?" asked my mother, **puzzled**.

But Flippi had seen through me **in a flash**. She **launched** straight into **an attack**. "You gave my snail to Lucilla to eat? Are you crazy? Do you know how difficult it is to find snails?" She jumped to her feet and came up to me **ominously**.

"Hey, hey, calm down!" I cried. "That's what happens when you put snails in my rucksack!"

"I didn't put any snails in your rucksack! How did you come up with such a stupid idea?"

---

meaningful – bedeutungsvoll, vielsagend; remorse – Reue;
poor devil – armer Kerl; on purpose – absichtlich;
to leap to one's defence – sich verteidigen;
puzzled – irritiert; in a flash – blitzschnell;
to launch an attack – einen Angriff unternehmen;
ominous – bedrohlich

"Oh, come on, Flippi! There was a snail invasion of my rucksack only a few days ago!"

"It was part of the **assault course**! The snails need it for training. And I gave your stupid rucksack back to you, didn't I?"

"Exactly. And you must have forgotten Fred."

"No, I didn't!"

Flippi's **denial** made me feel unsure.

"Mummyyyy!" Flippi cried for help. "Tell Jojo she should bring Fred back right now!"

My mum put on her strict face. "Well, really, Jojo, I find that quite **ridiculous**. **Playing pranks** like this at your age!"

"I haven't got Fred!"

"Oh, great! Because Lucilla ate him!" insisted Flippi.

I turned to my mother. "Mum, say something!"

"That's **revolting**," she replied with a **shudder**.

"But it's not true. Lucilla didn't eat Fred!"

My mother sighed. "Now stop arguing, you two. Jojo, please give Fred back to Flippi. And in future leave Flippi's snails alone."

Yeah, right, as if snails were right at the top of my wish list.

Flippi crossed her arms and looked at me provocatively.

I couldn't believe it. Why was this happening to

---

assault course – Übungsgelände; denial – Leugnen; ridiculous – albern; to play a prank – einen Streich spielen; revolting – ekelig; shudder – Schauder

me? What had I done? I didn't have anything to do with it! And where was I meant to find Fred?

Oh well, I thought, it can't be that difficult to find a snail. I mean, it doesn't really have to be Fred.

"And don't even think about looking for just any old snail. I can recognize Fred immediately!" warned Flippi as if she had **read my mind**.

Marvellous! All that before I'd even had breakfast!

And Fred wasn't my only problem. I still had to talk to Lucilla.

But at least I was in just the right bad mood as I **set off** for school. I decided to **go** straight **for the jugular**.

"Listen, Lucilla I need to talk to you," I said as soon as I saw her in front of school. "Don't you find it a bit **annoying** always being with me and Sven?"

Lucilla gave me a warm smile and **hugged** me. "That's so sweet of you, Jojo."

I swallowed. Why was I always talking such rubbish? What did I say that could be so easily **misinterpreted**?

"Don't worry about me," continued Lucilla, "I can **cope** with always being confronted by your happiness."

---

to read sb's mind – jmds. Gedanken lesen;
marvellous – klasse; to set off – sich aufmachen;
to go for the jugular – an die Gurgel springen;
annoying – ärgerlich; to hug – umarmen;
to misinterpret – missverstehen; to cope – zurechtkommen

I still hadn't understood. Whenever Lucilla starts to talk clever, I have no idea what she means.

Lucilla had a dreamy look in her eyes. "I just think of Niko."

"Oh?"

Lucilla sighed theatrically.

Niko is one of Sven's cousins. Lucilla met him at the masked ball on New Year's Eve. Niko is, in my opinion, a perfectly nice guy, it's just that he has the big **disadvantage** of not living here. He lives a long way away.

"Why Niko? Why do you think of him?" I asked in amazement.

"Oh, simple really," explained Lucilla. "You know, I always ask myself: And who loves me? Then I give myself an answer: Niko!"

"Why Niko?"

"Niko is my **Prince Charming**," **chirped** Lucilla. "And besides," she added **objectively**, "he's the only boy I've ever had a date with."

Well, a "date" is slightly **exaggerated**. Sven brought Niko with him to the masked ball. Lucilla and Niko met there for the first time and have never seen each other since.

"But Niko doesn't even live here!" I reminded Lucilla. "You hardly know him."

"Yes, that's right," smiled Lucilla, "isn't that

---

disadvantage – Nachteil; Prince Charming – Märchenprinz; to chirp – zwitschern; objective – sachlich; exaggerated – übertrieben totally romantic? We only had that one single evening together, but that was enough." She put her hand gently onto her heart and sighed, "He's the man of my dreams."

"Does he know that?" I asked.

"Of course he does. He can feel it."

"Oh, come on, Lucilla! He's a *boy*!" I reminded her. "Boys don't feel things like that. They could run into it **head first** and they wouldn't even notice!"

"Niko's different," said Lucilla, all smiles.

"Do you write to each other? Do you call?"

Lucilla was still smiling **serenely** and shook her head. "We don't need words." Then she thought about this for a second. "Perhaps that's the problem with your relationship, Jojo. You talk too much."

I **gasped**. The one and only problem in my relationship with Sven is Lucilla. And if I don't get it under control soon, somehow, then the problem will find another **solution**: that is, there won't even be a relationship between me and Sven any more.

I took a deep breath. "Lucilla, you need a boyfriend!" I said **resolutely**.

Lucilla looked at me with wide-open eyes full of horror. "But I have a boyfriend! Niko!"

"No, I mean a real boyfriend. One who lives here."

---

head first – Hals über Kopf; serene – selig;
to gasp – nach Luft schnappen; solution – Lösung;
resolute – entschlossen

“Oh, and **drop** Niko just like that? Jojo, you’re so **heartless**!”

“But the whole thing doesn’t stand a chance. Your relationship, I mean. If you can call it that. It isn’t really one, and it can’t become one either, because you never see each other!” And **in my mind** I added: nor write, nor call.

Lucilla looked at me, her eyes full of sadness. “What are you trying to say, Jojo? Are you trying to ruin my relationship with Niko? That’s not fair. I never stick my nose into your business with Sven!”

I bit my tongue. There was no way I could say what I really thought about that. Instead I just said, “I was only trying to help. I just think you need a real boyfriend. One who you can meet up with and go out with. Stuff like that. Then you won’t be the **raspberry** any more and always say: ‘And who loves me?’”

“I think the expression is ‘**gooseberry**’. I won’t be the gooseberry any more …”

“Raspberry, gooseberry, whatever! The main thing is you don’t feel like a **strawberry** any more.”

Lucilla looked at me for a while, then she asked, “Uhm, Jojo, do you have a problem with me going out with you and Sven?”

Right, there we were. It had finally come to this. All I had to do now was say “yes”.

---

to drop sb – jmdn. sitzen lassen; heartless – herzlos; in one’s mind – in Gedanken; raspberry – Himbeere; to be the gooseberry – das fünfte Rad am Wagen sein; strawberry – Erdbeere

And what did I say? "Of course not, Lucilla! What makes you think that?"

And to **dismiss** any **suspicion**, I invited her to come shopping with me and Sven the next afternoon.

Well, great. That went well. Congratulations, Jojo!

Friday 12th January

It's difficult to imagine quite how incredibly stupid my sister Flippi is.

I wake up in the middle of the night in an absolute panic because someone is shining my desk lamp into my face.

"Where's Fred?" says a humming voice.

I was so **sleepy** at first that I had no idea what was going on.

"You're better off **confessing**; otherwise we'll have to get nasty, sweetheart!"

Then I knew perfectly well who was standing behind the light.

"Flippi!" I cried furiously. "Are you **off your rocker**?"

---

to dismiss – abweisen, *hier:* zerstreuen;
suspicion – Verdacht; sleepy – schlaftrunken;
to confess – gestehen;
to be off one's rocker – übergeschnappt sein

"No excuses. I want the truth."

I sat up in bed and tried to get the lamp away from her. There was a **tussle** and the lamp fell to the floor.

"Man, Jojo!" cursed Flippi in the dark. "You've broken my **interrogation** lamp!"

I **groped** for the **light switch**, turned on my bed-side lamp and looked at the clock. "Flippi, you banana brain! It's 5 o'clock in the morning!"

"Correct. Don't you think I know that? I set my alarm clock especially." Flippi giggled. "It was good, wasn't it? I've always wanted to do something like that."

"At 5 in the morning?!" I couldn't believe it.

"You think I like doing things like this?" Flippi grumbled back. Then she giggled again. "Oh, I do, actually. It's great fun."

"Get out of my room! Right now!"

Flippi was **disappointed**. "You really are a **spoil-sport**, Jojo."

"Get out!" I shouted and threw my alarm clock at her.

"Thanks," said Flippi, catching my alarm clock **casually** and leaving the room with it.

Feeling exhausted, I threw myself back onto my pillows and groaned.

---

tussle – Gerangel; interrogation – Verhör;
to grope – tappen; light switch – Lichtschalter;
disappointed – enttäuscht; spoilsport – Spielverderber;
casual – lässig

Mum would have to make a decision: me or Flippi. Things just can't go on like this.

I gave my mum the ultimatum before breakfast, but she didn't seem to want to choose between us.

"Sit down, Jojo. I'll make you a cup of tea."

"I don't want a cup of tea. I just want to be an only child!"

The doorbell rang and interrupted our discussion.

Oskar is my mum's boyfriend. Ever since my dad ran off, Oskar has looked after us and Mum. He's a **scenery painter** in the theatre where Mum works as a costume designer. That is, I wish she worked there, but most of the time she works from home. "I can't leave the kids alone all day," is her main reason for doing this.

She takes her job as a Mum pretty seriously. Too seriously for my **taste**. She always reads the **Motherhood Manual** and tries out new methods for **bringing up** children. Since this often has to do with very **contradictory** theories, she keeps making U-turns which **quite frankly** leave me feeling **dizzy**. As soon as I've got used to being treated in such a way as to allow me all the freedom in the world, so that I learn to make independent decisions, a new theory

---

scenery painter – Kulissenmaler; taste – Geschmack;
motherhood manual – Erziehungsratgeber;
to bring up – erziehen; contradictory – widersprüchlich;
quite frankly – offen gesagt; dizzy – schwindlig

comes along saying children need **limits** and Mum starts making rules and **interfering** in my life.

The whole thing leaves me feeling so **confused**, I sometimes don't even know what my name is.

Flippi is completely **impervious** to all this. She just does what she wants, no matter what.

"Morning, girls!" said Oskar as he greeted us. "Isolde, we have to leave," he said, turning to my mother. Then he checked our packed lunches. "Wow, **wholemeal bread** with a vegetable **spread**." He pulled a face. "Ever heard of a **balanced diet**?" he asked my mother.

My mother looked **alarmed**.

Oskar pulled two **chocolate bars** out of his pocket and put them into our boxes. "For school you need something for the nerves," he explained and **winked** at us.

My mother was **utterly** baffled. Flippi took both the chocolate bars and walked out of the door.

"Hey!" I called after her, but Oskar held me back, took another chocolate bar out of his pocket and gave it to me.

My mum **was caught** completely **unawares** and didn't put up the slightest fight.

---

limit – Grenze; to interfere – sich einmischen;
confused – verwirrt; impervious – unempfindlich;
wholemeal bread – Vollkornbrot; spread – Aufstrich;
balanced diet – ausgewogene Ernährung;
alarmed – erschrocken; chocolate bar – Schokoriegel;
to wink – zwinkern; utterly – völlig;
to catch sb unawares – jmdn. überrumpeln

As I went out of the kitchen, I heard her saying to Oskar, “And who’s going to eat the sandwiches now?”

“Us.”

“You must be joking! They taste awful!” replied my mum, **horrified**. “Have you got another chocolate bar?”

Well, bravo. I won’t comment on that one.

My afternoon wasn’t much better either.

While Sven and I were waiting for Lucilla in the shopping centre, I gave Sven a lecture about how it should be a problem for him going out with two girls at the same time and told him that it was up to him to do something about it.

But he refused to agree with me.

“Jojo, I really think that’s your problem.”

“Hm. But can I at least tell Lucilla that it’s getting on your nerves and that you don’t want to have her around any more?”

Sven looked at me and grinned. “Great! Then you’ll have done exactly the thing you wanted to avoid.”

“What?”

“Then you’ll have dumped your best friend because of some guy.”

“That’s just **splitting hairs**!” I said, getting annoyed. “You’re really not being very helpful … ”

---

horrified – entsetzt;
to split hairs – Haarspalterei betreiben

Sven laughed. “If I let you talk for a few more minutes, then you’ll probably start telling me it’s all my fault.”

“Oh? And how are you going to stop me from doing that?” I asked, looking for a fight.

Sven had the ultimate solution: he kissed me.

“And who’s going to kiss me?” asked Lucilla.

I **spun around**. “Sorry! I didn’t see you coming,” I mumbled, feeling guilty.

“I would offer you a **frog**, but I don’t happen to have one with me,” said Sven cheerfully to Lucilla, looking through his pockets. Then he pointed at my rucksack. “But maybe Jojo has got a **spare** snail!”

“Very funny!” was I all I could say.

Lucilla laughed. “It was so funny, the way you screamed in the middle of the concert, and then …” she was laughing so much she could hardly talk, “… and all because of a wine gum …”

“It was a snail,” I interrupted her, annoyed.

“Says who?” **intervened** Sven.

“Flippi. She’s lost Fred. The thing I threw across the concert hall was one of her snails.”

Sven laughed and shook his head. “**Nonsense**. It was a wine gum.”

“No, it was Fred.”

“Oh my God!” All of a sudden, Lucilla turned pale. “And I ate him!”

---

to spin around – herumfahren; frog – Frosch;
spare – Ersatz-; to intervene – eingreifen;
nonsense – Unsinn

The corners of Sven's mouth were **twitching** with laughter. He gave a quick grin but then decided to calm Lucilla down. "It was a wine gum, believe me, Lucilla."

"Are you sure?"

Sven nodded and gave me a look that said I should keep my mouth shut.

"Jojo wanted to talk to you about something," said Sven to Lucilla, changing the **subject**.

"You're impossible!" I **snapped at** Sven.

But Sven just grinned.

"What is it?" asked Lucilla **curiously**.

I turned red. Sven just waited for me to say something with a big grin on his face. I refused to speak and just stared at him **defiantly**.

Sven looked at me kind-heartedly. I suppose he meant well.

Urgh, I really can't stand it when people mean well with me. But I couldn't be angry with Sven, even though I really tried.

"So," Lucilla asked me with big, **innocent** eyes. "What's this about? How can I help you?"

I pulled a face. "By giving me a million euros and an **escape car**?" I tried.

Sven shook his head and laughed. "Anything else?"

---

to twitch – zucken; subject – Thema;
to snap at sb – jmdn. anfauchen; curious – neugierig;
defiant – trotzig; innocent – unschuldig;
escape car – Fluchtwagen

"A Hawaii pizza?"

Sven laughed again and gave me a hug.

"Never do anything like that again," I hissed to him quietly.

"**Coward**," he whispered back.

"I have no idea what's going on here," commented Lucilla.

I giggled. Sven laughed and kissed me.

"Really Sven!" said Lucilla, **telling** Sven **off** for kissing me.

Sven raised his hands **apologetically**. "Don't say anything, Lucilla. I **plead guilty**!"

Lucilla looked slightly **taken aback**.

Sven pointed to the **butcher's** behind us. "A crime against romance …" he continued guiltily "… kissing in front of a meat shop!"

Lucilla giggled at Sven. "You're impossible!" she sighed. "So, what are we going to do now?"

"I suggest that as a specialist in romance you, Lucilla, show me a place where I can kiss Jojo," said Sven and made **a sweeping gesture** around the shopping centre.

Lucilla looked around, searching for a **suitable**

---

coward – Feigling; to tell sb off – jmdn. ausschimpfen;
apologetic – entschuldigend;
to plead guilty – sich schuldig bekennen;
taken aback – überrascht;
butcher's – Metzgerei;
a sweeping gesture – eine ausholende Geste;
suitable – geeignet, passend

place. Then she looked at Sven **suspiciously**. “Are you **taking the mickey out of** me?”

“Only a bit,” Sven **reassured** her. “Come on, I’ll buy you both a Coke.”

We started heading towards the ice-cream shop. I gave a sigh.

“Talk to her,” Sven whispered to me.

He was right. I had to tell Lucilla **in no uncertain terms** that I wanted to be alone with Sven. But how could I say that without hurting her feelings?

The best thing would be if she decided for herself not to go out with us all the time. She needs her own life and her own boyfriend. If only she wasn’t so horribly in love with Niko. Niko lives just too far away. We need a Niko, here and now. Exactly.

I just have to make sure she falls in love with another boy. That can’t be all that difficult, can it?

All I have to do is look for a boyfriend for Lucilla. And then everybody will be happy. Having made this **decision**, I started to be in a really good mood again.

But that didn’t **last** for long. Carla and Marc came into the ice-cream shop. “Watch out, Marc, it’s Jojo!” said Carla sarcastically, when she caught sight of me. “Make sure she doesn’t jump on you again.”

---

suspicious – misstrauisch;
to take the mickey out of sb – jmdn. aufziehen;
to reassure – beruhigen;
in no uncertain terms – klar und deutlich;
decision – Entscheidung; to last – dauern

Lucilla giggled.

I gave Lucilla my meanest look, but she just looked back at me innocently. She didn't **get** a thing. I did my "I-refuse-to-react-routine", which earned me a look of astonishment from Sven.

"Still got a guilty conscience about the rucksack episode?" he asked quietly.

I nodded. "But only until her hair has grown back," I replied in a whisper.

Sven nodded, relieved.

Lucilla budged up on the seat. "Do you want to join us?" she asked the **couple**.

Carla ignored Lucilla's offer. Marc was just about to **take** it **up**, but as he stepped towards us, Carla **tore** him back **roughly**.

I couldn't help grinning.

I suddenly had a thought: "Man! I need a snail. It's **urgent**!" I turned to Sven. "Where can I find a snail?"

Carla turned down the corners of her mouth, **revolted**, and looked for a table as far away from us as possible.

"In the **delicatessen**?" suggested Sven.

Haha! Very funny.

---

to get – *hier:* verstehen; couple – Paar;
to take up an offer – ein Angebot annehmen;
to tear – reißen; rough – grob; urgent – dringend;
revolted – angewidert; delicatessen – Feinkostgeschäft

Saturday 13th January

Finding a snail was no big deal. Not that it **solved** the problem. Sometimes you just have to sit things out and do nothing. There was the small **possibility** that Flippi might have forgotten about Fred.

The situation with Lucilla was much more important now, and my real problem was: Where could I find a boyfriend for her?

I **racked my brains**, but had no idea. I was in a really bad mood. I sat in the kitchen and **prodded** at my food.

"What's the matter, Jojo?" asked Mum. "Is something wrong with your lunch?" she asked alarmed. I could hear the **trace** of a guilty conscience in her voice.

She'd tried to make a lunch, but because she had absolutely no experience at all, it all **went pear-shaped**. Ignoring the problem of the taste – which is not difficult, because my mum's cooking is always taste-free – there was an **additional** problem with the "timing".

At 11 o'clock she put the sauce on the table for us. "The potatoes are coming in a second," she said as she started to **peel** the potatoes.

---

to solve – lösen; possibility – Möglichkeit;
to rack one's brains – sich den Kopf zerbrechen;
to prod – rumstochern; trace – Spur;
to go pear-shaped – schiefgehen;
additional – zusätzlich; to peel – schälen

"Are we having meat?" I asked.

My mum was completely taken aback. "**Good heavens**! I completely forgot to take it out of the **freezer**." She hurried over to the fridge, took a deep-frozen packet out and looked at it unhappily.

An hour later the potatoes arrived while we watched the meat **thaw**.

In the meantime Flippi had taken out a packet of cornflakes and milk, but Mum was quick to stop her. "You'll ruin your appetite," she said.

"That's the idea," **snarled** Flippi, casting a meaningful glance at the food.

"Well now," said my mum, **puffing herself up**, "other children would be happy if they ..."

"Mummy," whistled Flippi, **fluttering her eyelids**, "you're the best mum in the world and I love you. And if you love me, too, then let me eat my cornflakes."

Mum smiled, **reconciled**, and looked at Flippi dreamily as she tipped the cornflakes into a bowl and **poured** the milk on top.

I thought I would **take advantage of** the moment, so I grabbed the cornflakes packet and said, "I love you t ..."

Good heavens! – Du lieber Himmel!;
freezer – Gefrierschrank; to thaw – auftauen;
to snarl – knurren; to puff oneself up – sich aufplustern;
to flutter one's eyelids – mit den Wimpern klimpern;
reconciled – versöhnt; to pour – gießen;
to take advantage of – ausnutzen

But I wasn't even able to finish my sentence. "Take your hands off the cornflakes, Jojo. Lunch will be ready in a minute."

"I have no idea what you always do wrong," whispered Flippi without even looking up at me.

Flippi ate her cornflakes and left the kitchen without saying another word. Well, not quite. She managed to turn around to me and say **menacingly**, "Just one word: Where is Fred?"

At least I had the **presence of mind** to reply, "That was three words."

That left Flippi cold. "Snail-eater," she hissed and went into her room.

I sighed. So much for Flippi forgetting about Fred.

I **remained** seated in my chair like a good girl until Mum had ended her cooking experiment.

It was now 3 o'clock in the afternoon and I tried to cut the meat. It was still ice cold in parts.

For a while my mum watched my **efforts**. Eventually she said sheepishly, "You don't have to eat it, Jojo." She took my plate away and checked the temperature of the meat with her finger. "I really am a bad cook."

"Oh, you're not that bad," I tried to reassure her. "You're just ..."

"... a bad cook," added my mother.

---

menacing – drohend;
presence of mind – Geistesgegenwart;
to remain – bleiben; effort – Bemühung

"But you mean well," I tried to **comfort** her.

She gave me an unhappy look, stood up and made me a Nutella sandwich.

That's how Mum's cooking experiments always ended: Nutella sandwich or takeaway pizza. That day she was too **depressed** to call for takeaway pizza.

"So, what's the matter?" she asked as she gave me my sandwich. "You've got a problem!"

"No, don't worry. Everything's fine."

Or should I talk to her about it?

"Oh," I sighed, "you know, Lucilla needs a –" I stopped in mid-sentence. For some reason it didn't feel right telling my mum about this.

"What does Lucilla need?" she asked curiously.

"A ... a ... bicycle. Lucilla needs a bicycle."

"But she's already got one."

"Yes, she has, but it's too far away."

Huh? That **made** no **sense**.

"Why is her bike too far away?"

"No, I mean, she needs another bike."

"New or used?"

I had to smile. "What's the difference?" I asked, playing innocent.

My mother shook her head. "The price, of course!" she said, taken aback.

I **snorted with laughter**.

"What's the matter, Jojo?"

---

to comfort – trösten; depressed – deprimiert;
to make sense – Sinn ergeben;
to snort with laughter – losprusten

"Nothing, everything's fine. I'm sorry. I'm a bit silly today."

My mum shook her head, **mumbled** something that sounded like "puberty" and "teenager" and then started to clean up the kitchen. That is, she threw her food into the **bin**. I was expecting the bin to **spit out** the food in horror, but my mum quickly shut the **lid**. She probably was thinking the same as I was.

She sighed.

"Oskar?" I asked. And then I suddenly realized why the food today was such a complete disaster. Mum always needed maximum concentration and the best possible mood to cook. It **raised** the chances of the food being edible.

"Yes," she replied **briefly**.

"Did he ...?"

"Yes, he did!" She spun around and hurled the kitchen towel furiously into the sink. "He just can't **kick the habit**! He introduced me to some guy in **props** today and said I was his wife. When he saw I was angry, he corrected himself and said, 'My *future* wife'."

Now it was my turn to sigh. Mum is pretty complicated. Oskar's only **crime** is that he wants to marry

---

to mumble – murmeln; bin – Mülleimer;
to spit out – ausspucken; lid – Deckel;
to raise – steigern; brief – kurz;
to kick a habit – sich etwas abgewöhnen;
props – Requisiten; crime – Verbrechen

my mum and from time to time he **proposes** to her. Every time he does this, my mum takes it as a sign that he doesn't **take** her wishes and feelings **into consideration**. In other words, that he doesn't love her. She's "through with the matter" as she likes to say. Marriage is quite out of the question. Hardly surprising after the disaster with my father. But that doesn't mean she can start a huge **argument** with Oskar each time he **mentions** the word. She's **over-the-top** about it. And Oskar is quite simply a hopeless romantic.

"You know ..." my mum started to say.

All of a sudden, I had a thought that I couldn't wait to get rid of. "There's something I wanted to ask you: where would you look for a *bicycle*?"

At first my mum looked slightly confused, then offended and finally said rather **curtly**, "You can find a new one in a bike shop. Or a used one in the newspaper." Then she fell silent, turned around and threw all the **pots and pans** angrily into the dishwasher.

Oh yeah, great idea. Let's go to a bike shop and ask if they've got a boyfriend for Lucilla. Though a used boyfriend would be fine. Then we might as well just take a look in the newspaper. Hahaha!

---

to propose – einen Heiratsantrag machen;
to take sth into consideration – etwas berücksichtigen;
argument – Streit; to mention – erwähnen;
over-the-top – übertrieben; curt – schroff;
pots and pans – Töpfe und Pfannen

Just a moment. That's not such a bad idea. I don't mean the bike shop, I mean the newspaper.

Couldn't I find a boyfriend for Lucilla in the newspaper? There are always those **personal ads**.

I went and found all our old newspapers and started looking through them.

Unfortunately, I didn't find anything. No 15-year-old boys looking for a 13-year-old girlfriend.

Shame. It would just have been too easy.

My mum had finished cleaning up and wanted to go. "Is there anything else I can do for you?" she asked me curtly.

"Sorry, Mum."

She waved her hand dismissively. She wasn't angry with me any more. "It's okay. I was thinking: Lucilla could always put in her own ad for the bicycle, of course."

I looked at my mother in astonishment. Then I gave her a big smile and hugged her. "You're fantastic! What a great idea! An advertisement! Of course."

And **without further ado** I disappeared into my room and started to **draft** an advertisement.

In a few days everything will be just perfect. Lucilla will have a boyfriend and I will have my **peace and quiet**.

---

personal ad – Kontaktanzeige; Shame. – *hier:* Schade.;
without further ado – ohne Weiteres;
to draft – entwerfen; peace and quiet – Ruhe

Monday 15th January

I was in a really good mood as I jumped out of bed this morning.

'Today will change my life!' I thought and **rushed** out of my room into the kitchen. Lucilla's advertisement would be in the newspaper already.

I looked through the newspaper hectically, but I couldn't find anything. Nothing at all. **Zilch**. Niente. Nada. This couldn't be true! The advertisement was meant to **appear** today. What had gone wrong?!

The phone rang.

Mum looked surprised. "So early in the morning?"

Then she **spotted** Flippi. Flippi was in the middle of **carrying out** her **customary** breakfast procedure: one hand in the cornflakes packet up to her elbow, the other hand pouring herself a glass of milk.

"What have you **been up to**, Flippi?"

Flippi looked **incensed**. "How am I meant to know?" she said, **stuffing** a handful of cornflakes into her mouth, taking a **gulp** of milk and shaking her head to mix it all up in her mouth.

Flippi's outrage was **justified**. She was the cause

---

to rush – eilen; zilch – nix; to appear – erscheinen;
to spot – sehen; to carry out – durchführen;
customary – üblich; to be up to sth – etwas anstellen;
incensed – empört; to stuff – stopfen;
gulp – Schluck; justified – gerechtfertigt

of so much chaos and so many disasters that it would have been asking too much for her to keep an **overview**.

"Can't you eat properly, Flippi?" complained Mum.

Flippi was polite enough not to answer with her mouth full.

I ran to the telephone.

"Yes, good morning, I'm calling about the advertisement," said a friendly voice on the other end of the **line**.

I was baffled. So the advertisement had been printed after all! I must have missed it.

"Yes?" I asked, full of hope, although I was rather surprised because the voice belonged to an old lady rather than a cool guy.

"Well, we have a rabbit."

"A what?" I cried.

"A black one. With a white **patch** on its left ear."

"A rabbit?" I asked **in disbelief**.

"It's very friendly. It's never bitten anyone."

I could only repeat myself. "A rabbit?"

"Would you rather have a dog?" asked the nice lady.

"No, thank you! I'm looking for a boy," I cried **candidly**.

"A boy dog or a boy rabbit?" the lady asked.

---

overview – Überblick; line – Leitung; patch – Fleck;
in disbelief – ungläubig;
candid – ehrlich

"No, no. I mean a **male** friend."

"Yes, I read that. But you didn't write which animal or **breed** the friend should be."

I **beg your pardon**? What's going on here?

"Just a moment. Could you just hold the line?" I cried into the phone, rushed into the kitchen and tore the newspaper out of my mum's hand.

I looked through the paper again with a sense of panic. No. Nothing. No advertisement under "personals". But no! There it was! Hey, but what's that??!!

"Pets section." It had been printed under the category "Pets section".

I can't believe it. I'm actually looking for a boyfriend for Lucilla in the pets section?! Oh, man!

My carefully written advertisement was **unmistakeable**: ***Faithful*** *friend* ***sought*** *for* ***companionship****. Preferably sweet and loyal with beautiful eyes made for moonlit walks. No* ***flies on the wall****, please!*

Damn, damn, damn. This couldn't be true. My ad sounded like I was looking for a dog. With a bit of imagination it could be a rabbit, too. But at least I could count on not getting any calls from a fly-breeder. Hahaha.

My whole plan is **down the drain**! No boyfriend for Lucilla! All I can give Lucilla now is a rabbit.

---

male – männlich; breed – Rasse;
I beg your pardon? – Wie bitte?;
unmistakeable – unverkennbar; faithful – treu;
sought – gesucht; companionship – Freundschaft;
to be a fly on the wall – Mäuschen spielen;
to go down the drain – vor die Hunde gehen

Well, congratulations, Lucilla will be happy about that! Especially since she doesn't even want a boyfriend **in the first place**. I'll have to think of something. I can't have spent all that money on the ad for nothing. But I had an idea immediately.

I rushed back to the telephone.

"Sorry to keep you waiting, it's me again," I **stuttered** into the telephone quite **out of breath.** "Do you have any children?"

"Two," replied the woman sounding slightly astonished.

"Boys or girls?"

"Both boys."

"How old are they?"

"Twelve and 14."

Lucilla is 13. So we'll take the 14-year-old.

"Okay." I knew what I had to do. "I'm interested in the rabbit. Could your son … er … the older one, please … could he meet up with me so that I can take a look at him?"

"I beg your pardon?"

"I mean, the rabbit," I quickly corrected myself, "I'd like to take a look at the rabbit, if that's okay. Perhaps your son could … come with the rabbit …"

The woman was **obviously** feeling rather **doubtful** now. "I don't know …" she interrupted me.

---

in the first place – in erster Linie;
to stutter – stottern; out of breath – außer Atem;
obvious – offensichtlich; doubtful – zweifelnd

"Wouldn't it be better if you came around here with your son or daughter ...?"

"I am my daughter. I mean, I'm not my mother. Look, I'm just me."

God, that was **messy**. I was starting to panic. I wanted to make sure I didn't **blow it** with the woman. I mean, how often do you find someone who not only has a rabbit **on offer**, but also a 14-year-old son?!

The woman was looking to end the conversation. "Why don't you think it over and give me a call back?"

"No! Just tell me when I can come around."

"Thursday at 3 o'clock?"

"Fine." I took down the address and hung up.

Then I **jumped out of my skin**: my mum was standing behind me like the **avenging angel**.

I made sure I looked as innocent as possible. "What's the matter?" I asked her as innocently as possible.

"That's exactly what I wanted to ask you!" she said, snapping the newspaper out of my hand.

I shrugged my shoulders. "It's for Lucilla. She's looking for a ... rabbit," I lied.

"I thought she was looking for a bicycle?"

Oh, yeah, of course!

---

messy – unerfreulich; to blow it – etwas vermasseln;
on offer – im Angebot;
to jump out of one's skin – erschreckt hochfahren;
avenging angel – Racheengel

"Exactly! A bicycle! That's what I meant! You said we should put an advertisement in the newspaper."

"Jojo ..." My mother sounded rather **concerned**, "... what's the matter? Something is wrong."

I opened my eyes wide, pretending to be amazed. "What makes you think that? Oh, come on, Mum, you know me!"

"Exactly."

Ouch, that was an **own goal**.

My mum put her hand on my shoulder and moved into the mother-daughter-conversation-position.

I just managed to get away in time. "I have to go to school. Bye!" I called and ran.

I heard my mum sigh behind me. Flippi **yelled** after me. "Don't forget Fred!"

Monday evening, 15th January

Flippi's words were still **ringing** in my ears as school ended and I walked over to Sven's school to wait for him. We always do that. **Whoever** finishes first **picks up** the other.

Sven was going to have to help me find a snail.

---

concerned – beunruhigt;
own goal – Eigentor; to yell – schreien;
to ring – schallen; whoever – wer auch immer;
to pick up – abholen

"Have you got time today?" I asked him.

"For you or for Lucilla?"

"What's that supposed to mean?"

"Listen," he said, playing around again, "I have a **reputation** to look after. I can't be seen going out with two girls at the same time. So just tell me who I'm going out with today and I'll tell you if I have time."

"Sven, I'm in the middle of solving our problem!" I told him. "I now know what we have to do."

"*We* don't have to do anything. *You* have to talk to Lucilla. It's as simple as that."

"Yeah, yeah. Just listen to me for a second, will you? I've got a great idea: I'm going to find a boyfriend for Lucilla. Then she'll stop **hanging around** with us."

Sven didn't say a word.

"What do you think of my idea?"

"The idea isn't bad. The only problem is: it's one of yours. It will all end in complete disaster!"

"How can you say a thing like that?!"

Sven laughed. "Just being realistic."

"Have you got time this afternoon or not?" I repeated my **initial** question.

"To be honest, the risk of having to spend the afternoon with a giggling Lucilla and a **bad-tempered** Jojo is just too great."

---

reputation – Ruf; to hang around – rumhängen;
initial – ursprünglich;
bad-tempered – schlecht gelaunt

"Nonsense. The problem with Lucilla is almost as good as solved."

"Then give me a call when it *is* solved," he suggested in a friendly way.

"Maybe I won't call you at all – ever!" I snapped back **tersely**.

"Then I'll call you."

"I won't answer the phone."

"How will you know it's me calling?"

"I can tell by the ring," I **claimed**.

Sven laughed. "You're really sweet, Jojo!"

"Really?" I asked, sensing **reconciliation**.

"Yes."

"How sweet?"

"What **choices** do I have?"

"As sweet as **candyfloss**, strawberry bonbons or chocolate?"

"As sweet as a **gherkin**."

"That wasn't on the list. And gherkins aren't sweet."

"Yes, they are. **Bittersweet**. That **fits**."

Oh boy, things always start so **promisingly** with Sven. Then he always says something which completely kills the romance. Lucilla's right.

---

terse – knapp; to claim – behaupten;
reconciliation – Versöhnung; choice – Wahl;
candyfloss – Zuckerwatte;
gherkin – Essiggurke;
bittersweet – süßsauer; to fit – passen;
promising – vielversprechend

I sighed. Now I had to talk about the even more urgent matter.

"Listen, Sven, I need to find a snail."

"I wish I had your problems."

"**Be my guest**! Find me a snail!"

"Put a missing snail ad in the newspaper," grinned Sven.

"Stop being silly!"

Hold on a moment, we already had that one. Who knows? Maybe someone was trying to call me right that minute. Someone with a snail on offer! I had to get home.

"I have to go!" I cried to the baffled Sven and rushed home like a cat on fire.

A lot more calls really did come. For animals. Unfortunately, nobody had a snail he wanted to get rid off. Some callers even hung up when I said I was looking for a snail.

In the evening Sven came around again. With a small box.

"Here. It's for you."

"What is it?" I asked **inquisitively**.

"A sign of my love," he said dramatically.

I went all warm inside and turned red. Sven is sooo sweet. He really is romantic. I **have no idea** what Lucilla is talking about!!!

Be my guest! – Nur zu!;
inquisitive – neugierig;
to have no idea – keine Ahnung haben

I opened the little box, my heart **beating** like mad. Then I screamed and hurled the box away. It flew across the room in an **arc**.

What was inside? A snail, of course.

"Hey! Be a bit more careful with my presents," Sven had a go at me as he picked up the box and snail.

"What a stupid idea! What made you come up with that? Who wants a snail as a present?" I grumbled, still in shock.

"You. You said this afternoon that you needed one urgently."

Oh, right. Yes. That's true. Unfortunately. Although it was really nice of Sven to have helped me, I was still angry. Or more disappointed. Sven really is unromantic.

"Flippiiii!" I yelled through her closed door.

When Flippi turned up, I gave her the little box. She was over the moon.

"It's not Fred," I said, trying to bring her down.

"I can see that myself. **Who cares?** She's great. Where did you get her?" she turned to Sven.

"What makes you think Sven got her?" I asked **in a huff**.

Flippi just gave me a **pitiful** look and turned to Sven inquisitively.

---

to beat – schlagen; arc – Bogen;
Who cares? – Ist doch egal!;
in a huff – eingeschnappt;
pitiful – mitleidig

"A friend of mine has a terrarium. There are a few snails in it as well," he explained.

"Does your friend know that he's got one snail fewer now?" asked Flippi **tentatively**.

Sven **set her mind at rest**. "Yes, she does. No worries."

"Oh, I wasn't worried at all. I just wanted to know."

Sven grinned. Typical Flippi.

That was too much harmony for me. After all, Fred was still lost and Flippi had **insisted on** getting Fred back.

"And what about Fred?" I asked.

"Oh, forget about Fred!" Flippi waved dismissively. Then she gave Sven a big smile. "Thanks a lot. You're **alright**. **Apart from** the fact you like my sister."

Little **beast**! I was just about to say something when Flippi turned to me and said, "By the way, you still **owe** me Fred, don't forget that."

Then she rushed out of the door and my curses were **drowned out** by Sven's laughter.

---

tentative – vorsichtig;
to set sb's mind at rest – jmdn. beruhigen;
to insist on – bestehen auf;
alright – in Ordnung; apart from – abgesehen von;
beast – Biest; to owe – schulden;
to drown out – übertönen

Tuesday 16th January

I had a telephone call today from a guy offering to sell me a one-eyed frog. I tried to **engage him in a conversation** and find out how old he was – I mean, the guy not the frog – but he **misunderstood** me at first and said the frog was two years old and very friendly. **What's more**, he could whistle.

"What then?" I asked, interested.

"What do you mean 'what then'?"

"What song can he whistle?"

"Name one and he'll whistle it."

"Now? On the phone? I don't believe you."

"Of course he can. I just have to hold the phone up to him."

At that point I just hung up the phone without another word.

After all, I'm not doing this here for my own **pleasure**! I don't think people take advertisements like mine seriously enough!

Some people, however, took it **deadly seriously**. I'm now high up on the black list of the Friends and Supporters of the Fly-on-the-Wall-Breeders Association. A woman had a go at me and accused me of being anti-fly.

---

to engage sb in a conversation – jmdn. in ein Gespräch verwickeln;
to misunderstand – missverstehen;
what's more – außerdem;
pleasure – Vergnügen; deadly serious – todernst

I was thinking about asking for **police protection**. Boy, am I **at the end of my tether**.

I called Sven to tell him my **woes**.

"Guess what's happened ..." was the first thing I said.

"Fred called. He's sitting in Acapulco enjoying the good life on Flippi's pocket money," said Sven.

"Don't be silly. I'm talking about Lucilla's problem," I replied.

"If I know you, then you've already solved Lucilla's problem," said Sven **jovially**.

"That's right!" I replied immediately. I don't always let Sven **tease** me.

"Huh? You're not actually serious, are you? Did you buy yourself a special **recipe** and **bake** her a boyfriend?"

"Something along those lines," I said, feeling **uncomfortable**.

"Great. So that means we can meet up without somebody **constantly** telling us how and when to be romantic?"

"That's right." I had to stick to my story.

"Lucilla isn't going to be joining us any more?"

---

police protection – Polizeischutz;
to be at the end of one's tether – fertig mit den Nerven sein;
woe – Leid; jovial – gut gelaunt;
to tease – aufziehen;
recipe – Rezept; to bake – backen;
uncomfortable – unwohl; constant – dauernd

"Exactly."

What was I doing?! I was talking nonsense. I had actually wanted to tell Sven about how the advertisement had gone wrong. I'd wanted to tell him all about it. But somehow the conversation **had taken a turn** which I'd missed along the way, and now I couldn't tell the truth. Shame really.

"Okay then. To **celebrate,** why don't we go ice skating?!"

"I'm with you!" I said and felt a **pang** in my stomach. That's exactly where I was going to meet up with Lucilla.

Why couldn't I just go somewhere else with Sven? Why didn't I say anything to him?

Things were **heading for the rocks**, it was as clear as day. I had to do something to stop myself from **crashing**.

I called Lucilla straightaway and tried to **negotiate** not meeting up with her to go ice skating.

"Why not?" she asked.

"I don't feel like it. Let's go tomorrow."

"Okay."

Wow, that was easy.

I had to **make sure**. "So you're not going to go today without me?"

---

to take a turn – eine Wendung nehmen;
to celebrate – feiern; pang – plötzliches Schmerzgefühl;
to head for the rocks – ins Verderben rennen;
to crash – zusammenstoßen;
to negotiate – verhandeln; to make sure – sich versichern

"Yes, I am."

"Huh? Why? We just said we're going to go tomorrow."

"Yes, I know."

Either I'm confused or Lucilla is.

"So then let's go tomorrow!" I repeated.

"Yes, let's."

But for some reason I still wasn't **satisfied**. I had a bad feeling about this.

"And what are you doing today?" I asked, just to be on the safe side.

"I'm going ice skating," replied Lucilla.

"No!" I cried. Doesn't Lucilla understand anything? "I'm not going ice skating today," I cried **in despair**. "I'm going tomorrow! Okay?"

"Jojo, what on earth is the matter with you? I said I'll come with you tomorrow. Stop getting so worked up."

"But you just said you're going today."

"That's right. Today I'm going with Carla and her friends."

Oh no. Please no.

"Can't you **put** that **off**? Till tomorrow maybe?"

"But I'm going with you tomorrow!"

I gave up. It was making no sense talking to Lucilla like this. I had to call Sven and stop him.

I **dialled** his number and, as soon as someone

---

satisfied – zufrieden;
in despair – verzweifelt;
to put sth off – etwas verschieben; to dial – wählen

picked up the phone, I yelled, "No ice skating today!"

"Hello, Josefine. I hope you have a nice day, too."

Sven's mother. Why does this keep happening to me? I really must work on my telephone manners.

"Sorry. Is Sven still there?"

"No."

"**Blast**!" Whoops, not again! "Er, I mean, what a shame. And thank you very much, too. And I hope you have a nice day. And goodbye … er … all the best."

If I go on like this, she'll stop her son from seeing me.

I rushed off. I had to make an urgent **interception**. I had to stop Sven before he got to the **ice rink**.

Wednesday 17th January

Of course, by the time I finally got to the ice rink yesterday, Sven was already standing at the **ticket office**.

I threw my arms around his neck. "Ice skating is really **unhealthy**," I **puffed**, completely out of breath. "Let's do something else."

Blast! – Mist!; interception – Abfangen;
ice rink – Eishalle; ticket office – Kasse;
unhealthy – ungesund;
to puff – schnaufen

I tried to pull him away from the ticket office, but he didn't move a millimetre. He just looked at me and grinned.

"What is it?" I asked.

"I'm waiting," he said.

"What for?"

"You're in such a hurry to get away from here, something really embarrassing **is** probably **going to happen** any minute," he said with a smile, leaning casually against the ticket office.

"What could possibly happen? Nothing's going to happen. I'm just not in the mood for ice skating."

Sven thought about this for a second. "Does it have something to do with snails?"

"Not at all!"

He thought again. "I've got it! Lucilla! She's coming, too. And you still haven't talked to her about it. Right?"

"Wrong again."

Sven **pretended** to be really amazed. "How come? Doesn't she have any time today?" He pressed his hands to his heart and **wailed**, "She can't do this to me!"

I **gave him a nudge**. "Come on, stop being silly."

He put his arm around me and said, "I don't know how I can cope without her!" Then he bit my **earlobe**.

---

sth is going to happen – etwas muss passieren;
to pretend – vorgeben; to wail – jammern;
to give sb a nudge – jmdm. einen Stoß versetzen;
earlobe – Ohrläppchen

"Buy yourself a packet of crisps and leave my ear in peace," I told him off.

"Your earlobe isn't tasty anyway. It needs some ketchup."

Just then I happened to look over to the entrance and was shocked by what I saw: Lucilla. She was **heading towards** the ticket office with Carla and some friends.

Damn it! I frantically pulled Sven away from the ticket office.

"What's the matter?"

"I forgot something!" I said, while **inconspicuously** keeping an eye on Lucilla.

Sven followed my **line of sight** and saw Lucilla. Instinctively he took a step to one side and **took cover** with me behind an **advertising pillar**. We ducked down and looked over to Lucilla.

"You forgot to talk to Lucilla," **ascertained** Sven objectively.

I shrugged my shoulders with embarrassment. "Yes, well ..."

Sven just gave me a long, hard stare and said nothing.

"Are you angry?" I asked guiltily.

---

to head towards sth – auf etwas zusteuern;
inconspicuous – unauffällig;
line of sight – Blickrichtung;
to take cover – in Deckung gehen;
advertising pillar – Litfaßsäule;
to ascertain – feststellen

Sven was perfectly calm. “No,” he said with a grin. “I’ve always wanted to play Richard Kimble.”

“Who’s that?”

“A **fugitive**,” he said, putting on his film-hero face and pulling up his **collar**. “We’re **on the run**.”

I giggled.

Lucilla and the others bought their tickets and went into the ice rink.

Sven looked at his watch. “**Synchronize watches**. Okay. We’ve got about two hours. That is, two hours without Lucilla. Two completely unromantic hours,” said Sven full of **enthusiasm**. “Life loves us!”

He **crept** out from behind the advertising pillar, keeping his head down and pulling me with him.

“What are we going to do?” I asked.

“No idea, but – hey – the town **is our oyster**. We can go wherever we want. We’re in a Lucilla-free zone.”

Right then I was even more in love with Sven than I normally am. He’s sooo sweet!

All of a sudden, I had the feeling that everything would **turn out fine**. I just had to **hang on** until tomorrow when I would meet the rabbit boy and if

---

fugitive – Flüchtiger/Flüchtige;
collar – Kragen;
on the run – auf der Flucht;
to synchronize watches – einen Uhrenvergleich machen;
enthusiasm – Begeisterung; to creep – schleichen;
(the world) is sb’s oyster – jmdm. steht (die Welt) offen;
to turn out fine – gut ausgehen;
to hang on – durchhalten

he was any good, then the Lucilla problem would be a thing of the past.

Then I remembered my brilliant advertising idea. I really had to tell Sven about it.

I stopped, put my rucksack down on the ground and rummaged around for the newspaper with the advertisement. "What would you think of someone who came up with the **bright** idea of putting an advertisement in a newspaper to find a boyfriend?" I asked Sven.

"I'd think they were **as thick as two short planks**."

I **froze** in mid-movement. "I beg your pardon?"

Sven lifted his shoulders. "Well, come on, think about it … No normal person would **respond** to an advertisement like that!"

I quickly stuffed the newspaper back into my rucksack, but it was too late. Sven had already seen it.

He really ought to know me well enough not to ask the question: "You haven't, have you …?"

I stood up feeling outraged. "Of course I haven't! Who do you think I am?!" I said quickly.

Sven **stole a glance** at my rucksack. A corner of the newspaper was still showing. "Why have you got a newspaper in your bag?"

I looked tentatively at my rucksack.

---

bright – *hier:* schlau;
as thick as two short planks – dumm wie Stroh;
to freeze – erstarren; to respond – antworten;
to steal a glance – schielen

So what was the best option now: to say that it wasn't a newspaper or to say it wasn't my rucksack?

"It's a school project," I said **without a moment's hesitation**.

Sven looked at me out of the corner of his eye. "Are you sure you didn't **accidentally submit** a personal ad?"

Accidentally? I thought about this for a second. Could it **save my face**?

Sven looked at me very seriously. "Jojo, did you submit a personal ad for Lucilla?"

I said nothing. I hadn't **admitted** anything yet. Perhaps Sven would change the subject if I didn't say anything.

But he didn't. "You didn't give them Lucilla's address, did you? Or yours? There are a lot of freaks running around out there."

"Of course not!" I replied angrily. I just gave them my telephone number. No more. After all, it was urgent and when the woman at the newspaper asked me for my telephone number, I couldn't think of anything else. I just gave it to her without thinking about it. Until now. That wasn't the **smartest move**.

I started to feel slightly **uneasy**. At the same time

---

without a moment's hesitation – ohne eine Sekunde zu zögern; accidental – versehentlich; to submit – einreichen; to save one's face – das Gesicht wahren;
to admit – zugeben;
smart move – kluger Zug; uneasy – mulmig

I was angry with Sven. He could have told me that before. Why hadn't we talked about it in peace and quiet? Then he could have **talked me out of** it. Now it was too late. He didn't have to bother putting on that concerned **expression**.

Then I made a decision: "I didn't submit a personal ad." That was true. My ad was under "pets".

Sven was still looking at me **sceptically**. "And so why have I got such a strange feeling at the moment?"

"Because you're hungry. Come on, let's get you some chips with ketchup," I said, successfully **averting suspicion**.

Sven seemed to be relieved. He put his arm around me.

But I was in a bad mood. For some reason now I couldn't help thinking he was to blame for my misery.

---

to talk sb out of sth – jmdm. etwas ausreden;
expression – Gesichtsausdruck;
sceptical – misstrauisch;
to avert suspicion – *hier:* ablenken

Thursday 18th January

"Oh, Jojo, you really missed something yesterday," **reported** Lucilla before the first lesson this morning, obviously in a good mood. "It was so funny! Carla **did an impression of** you. She's a real **scream**."

"The idea of Carla doing an impression of me doesn't sound funny at all. You shouldn't laugh at things like that."

"Oh, she did an impression of me, too."

"That's really mean of her."

"Listen, I wanted to ask you: is it true you **wet the bed**?"

"Huh? What makes you think that?"

"Carla said so."

"That Carla is a **snake** with **poisonous fangs**! By the way, I'm not in the mood for ice skating today."

"Okay." After a short pause Lucilla asked, "Are you angry about something?"

"No."

"Is it something to do with Carla?"

"Not at all."

"Would you rather I didn't meet up with her?"

I looked at Lucilla pitifully. "That girl is really

---

to report – berichten;
to do an impression of sb – jmdn. nachahmen;
to be a scream – zum Schreien sein;
to wet the bed – bettnässen; snake – Schlange;
poisonous fang – Giftzahn

nasty. After all, I did apologize after the thing with the rucksack. And she's still mean to me. It really **winds** me **up**. And then there's you being friendly to her …"

Lucilla put her arm around me. "I don't really like her," she said. "She's just so cool. Everybody **admires** her. I don't actually want her as a friend."

Oh. Lucilla is such a nice person.

"And I don't care if you wet the bed."

I pushed Lucilla away from me. "Lucilla! Carla **made** that **up**! It's not true."

"Well, that's good. Just be **grateful** you don't do it."

Oh, man! And the day hadn't even begun yet. I thought about calling in sick and going home. Then I remembered just in time that my mum was at home for the whole morning.

At lunch Sven was waiting for me in front of school. A **ray of hope**.

"Shall we go for a pizza later?" he asked. "Incognito, of course." He rummaged about in his coat, pulled out a **fake moustache** and stuck it on. Then he took another moustache out of the other pocket

---

to wind sb up – *hier:* jmdn. auf die Palme bringen;
to admire – bewundern;
to make sth up – etwas erfinden;
grateful – dankbar;
ray of hope – Hoffnungsschimmer;
fake moustache – falscher Schnurrbart

and stuck it under my nose. "Nothing can go wrong now!"

"Well, apart from someone asking me if I want to join the Russian women's **discus** team."

"Just say 'njet'."

Sven walked me home and we had a lot of fun with our moustaches.

"So, see you later," said Sven. "I'll pick you up."

"Oh yes!" I replied full of enthusiasm. Wait a second! What about the rabbit boy?! "Oh no. I can't."

"Have you got a better plan?"

"Finding a boyfriend for Lucilla."

"That sounds better than having a boring old pizza with someone who's got a fake moustache stuck under their nose. Good luck!"

He kissed me goodbye. Our moustaches **got caught up** and I ended up having a double moustache. Neither Sven nor I noticed this at the time.

It was only when I went into the kitchen and my mum screamed when she saw me that I realized something was wrong.

Before I could explain, her eyes had that frightened-mother-look and she was putting the kettle on.

"Sit down, Jojo," she said, taking out the teabags. "I'll make us a cup of tea."

Not that as well. Other mums would have just said, "You've got a moustache under your nose,"

---

discus – Diskus;
to get caught up – sich verhaken

and that would have been the end of the matter. My mother makes me a cup of tea and wants to talk about it.

"You know, I think I'm a bit **out of my depth** with all your problems," she **whined**.

"I don't have any problems!" I tried to reassure her, but then I remembered what I was saying was about as true as the sun shining at night. I always have problems. My middle name is 'problem'.

"No, no, of course not," protested my mum at once. It was like she was scared I was going to **crack up** any second.

She took out two cups, poured hot water into them and put them on the kitchen table. The teabags remained **untouched** next to the kettle. Then she pushed me over to a chair and positioned herself opposite.

She smiled at me **meekly**, took a sip of hot water and continued to smile at me meekly. Boy, my moustache must have really got to her!

"Do you have a problem with your role as a woman?" asked my mother cautiously.

"No, but I do with the tea. I'm not into pure hot water."

---

to be out of one's depth – einer Sache nicht gewachsen sein;
to whine – jammern;
to crack up – überschnappen;
untouched – unberührt;
meek – sanftmütig

"Don't try and **sidetrack** me, Jojo," replied Mum, **unswerving**. She took another sip of her tea.

I took off the two moustaches and sat down. "Mum, it was just a joke."

My mother pulled a bittersweet face. "Strange **sense of humour**," she said. "Girls don't normally put on moustaches."

I **groaned**. "I'll never do it again, okay?"

"Now wait, if it's important to you then I don't want to stand in your way or anything like that ... " she said, suddenly remembering all the books she'd **avidly** read on how to bring up children.

I gave up. Then a **scalding hot** feeling came over me and I remembered the rabbit visit. I'd completely forgotten to **arrange** a time with Lucilla so that she could take a look at her candidate. I ran to the phone.

Mum was still confused. She called after me, "I'll always love you, whether you choose to wear a moustache or not!"

Well, I'm **glad** we cleared that one up!

I called Lucilla.

But what was happening? Lucilla wasn't in the mood. I couldn't believe it.

---

to sidetrack – ablenken; unswerving – unbeirrt;
sense of humour – Sinn für Humor;
to groan – stöhnen; avid – begeistert;
scalding hot – siedend heiß; to arrange – ausmachen;
to be glad – sich freuen, froh sein

"But you said yourself that you didn't want to do anything after school today," she reminded me.

"I changed my mind."

Lucilla didn't respond.

"You have to come with me!" I cried **in desperation**.

"I don't feel very well," she **moaned** into the phone. "I'm staying at home today."

I wish she said that more often when Sven and I went out together.

"But it's really important!" I **pleaded**.

"I'm not interested in rabbits. And anyway, since when have you been interested in them?"

"But I'm only doing it for you!" I cried in despair.

"For me? Jojo, what is the matter with you? I'm starting to get worried about you."

"Please come with me, Lucilla," I pleaded again.

"Jojo, haven't you got your own life? Go out with Sven, have a nice afternoon with him."

It was all going wrong.

"Jojo?"

"Yes."

"You're not angry with me now, are you?"

"Would that help **change your mind**?" I asked.

"No. I'm in a Niko mood today. I'm lying on the sofa, thinking of him."

I gave a loud groan.

---

in desperation – verzweifelt;
to moan – jammern; to plead – flehen;
to change one's mind – es sich anders überlegen

"Oh, Jojo, you just have no idea what it feels like to be in love!"

"No, of course not. How could I?" I snapped down the phone. Then I hung up.

Boy, I was angry! That **went smoothly** again. But what now? I'd **cancel** the meeting. No rabbit, no boyfriend for Lucilla. Why should I **care**? She can just go on dreaming of Niko.

The phone rang. Aha, Lucilla wanted to apologize.

But it wasn't her. It was the rabbit lady.

"Are we still meeting up?" she asked kindly.

"Of course," I replied without thinking.

Only after I'd hung up did I realize that I'd just missed the perfect **opportunity** to cancel.

But it was too late now. I'd arranged to meet up for the second time. It was all a **waste of time** really, but I **felt obliged** to take a look at the rabbit. Marvellous, now I'd have to go there on my own.

No, I didn't want to go completely alone. Someone had to come with me. As a kind of **camouflage**.

---

to go smoothly – glattgehen, glattlaufen;
to cancel – absagen;
to care – sich Gedanken machen;
opportunity – Gelegenheit;
waste of time – Zeitverschwendung;
to feel obliged – sich verpflichtet fühlen;
camouflage – Tarnung

I poked my head into Flippi's room. "How are you?"

Flippi looked at me suspiciously. "What do you want?"

"Nothing! Can't I even have a little **chat** with my sister without her **accusing** me of getting up to something bad?"

Flippi looked at me doubtfully. "Alright, get to the point: what do you want?"

"I just wanted to be nice!"

"Oh, come on, **that's a likely story**!"

What is wrong with this family? They have no **trust** in each other.

"You've got a guilty conscience!" **concluded** Flippi.

"Oh yeah? What about?"

"Because of Fred!"

I swallowed. "Well, to be honest ..." I was just about to tell Flippi the concert story, but then I decided to go for the short version. "I don't have Fred."

Flippi nodded. "I know."

"You know? What's that supposed to mean?"

Flippi shrugged her shoulders. "He didn't disappear in the first place. He was just hiding under a **lettuce leaf**."

---

chat – Schwatz;
to accuse – *hier:* unterstellen;
that's a likely story – wer's glaubt, wird selig;
trust – Vertrauen; to conclude – schlussfolgern;
lettuce leaf – Salatblatt

"Whaaat? You had him here all the time? And you didn't say anything? You even let Sven give you a new snail?!"

"Yes," said Flippi **bluntly**. "It was great to see you **squirm** and creep around with a guilty conscience all the time. And besides, I've got a new snail now. It was well **worth it**." And with that the matter was over.

"Oh, man, Flippi . . . " I started, but then I remembered that I was in a hurry to go to the rabbit lady and I still didn't want to go alone. Even Flippi was good enough for me. I swallowed my **anger** and smiled at my little sister. "Shall we go and look at some rabbits?"

"No."

"Rabbits are great."

"Can they do anything?"

"Of course."

"What?"

"All sorts of things."

"What then?"

"You can train them really well," I said. "They **fetch** things, chase off **intruders**, look after snails, things like that."

"You're talking about dogs."

---

blunt – direkt;
to squirm – sich winden;
to be worth it – sich lohnen;
anger – Ärger; to fetch – *hier:* apportieren;
intruder – Eindringling

"Rabbits and dogs are very **similar**. They've just got longer ears."

"Yeah, sure!"

Then I started **to lose my cool**. "Please, come with me!" I pleaded with Flippi.

"Wow," gasped Flippi in amazement. "Are you in trouble?"

"Of course not!"

Flippi looked at me sceptically.

"Don't you want a rabbit?" I asked her. I must have **taken leave of my senses**.

"Are you serious? Can I have one?"

"I don't have a problem with you having one," I said, but I was sure that Mum would.

Flippi **leant back** and looked at me. "You really want me to come with you, don't you?"

I nodded.

"How much is it worth?"

"What's that supposed to mean?"

"I'm easily bought," she **prompted** me.

"How much?" came my **reply**.

"Two euros."

"Okay."

"Okay?" said Flippi surprised. "Damn it! I should have said five euros!"

---

similar – ähnlich; to lose one's cool – die Nerven verlieren;
to take leave of one's senses – den Verstand verlieren;
to lean back – sich zurücklehnen;
to prompt sb – jmdm. auf die Sprünge helfen;
reply – Antwort

"Too late. Here's the money. Let's go."

Flippi's face lit up with a smile. "Okay, what are we waiting for? Off to the rabbits!"

That was the first time I had the feeling that maybe it wasn't such a good idea to take Flippi along.

We set off.

We got to the house and a woman answered the door. Flippi immediately spotted two boys standing behind her, a taller boy and a smaller boy, both pretty good-looking.

Flippi nudged me in the **ribs** and hissed, "That was a **nasty trick** to play on me. They're boys, not rabbits!"

Flippi's **dislike** of boys is well-known all over town. No boy from her class even dares to come into her **vicinity** any more **unless** he's master of at least seven different Asian martial arts.

"Hello," I **greeted** the lady politely while nudging Flippi back, "I'm Josefine, this is my little sister, Filipine."

"What are you doing?" hissed Flippi to me. "Our real names?"

I ignored her.

---

rib – Rippe;
nasty trick – mieser Trick;
dislike – Abneigung;
vicinity – Nähe; unless – es sei denn;
to greet – begrüßen

“Then come in and take a look at the rabbit,” said the lady in a friendly manner.

I gave Flippi a meaningful look. She just shrugged her shoulders apologetically.

She turned to her sons. “Come on, Moritz and Max, show the girls the rabbits!”

Flippi rolled her eyes. “Max and Moritz! Great!”

I looked at the two boys with interest, trying to make eye contact with the older one. I smiled at him with all the charm I could **muster**. He looked back at me **vacantly**. At least his little brother tried to smile.

The two boys **led** us into a hobby room in a cellar. For some reason I had a good feeling and so I spontaneously changed my mind: I decided to use the opportunity to look for a boyfriend for Lucilla. She didn’t actually **deserve** it, but I was **ultimately** doing it for me and Sven.

In the cellar there were a lot of rabbits hopping around.

The taller of the two boys fished a black animal out of the sea of animals and held it under my nose. “This is Blacky.”

I was looking at the guy, not the rabbit. “And what’s your name?”

“Moritz.”

“Which class are you in?”

---

to muster – aufbringen; vacant – geistesabwesend;
to lead – führen; to deserve – verdienen;
ultimately – letzten Endes

"Sixth grade."

"Sixth grade? How old are you then?"

"Twelve."

"Oh really? And why are you so tall?" I said reproachfully, but I didn't wait for his answer. There was no time to waste. "So you're the 14-year-old?" I turned to his brother who was a head smaller.

He nodded.

"And you're called Max," I remembered.

He nodded again.

"What are your hobbies?"

"Oh, I . . . "

"Are you looking for a rabbit or a boyfriend?" **butted in** Moritz all of a sudden.

I was completely **gobsmacked** by this **unabashed** question.

"Exactly!" Flippi butted in. "Let's take the **bunny** and get out of here."

Flippi was just about to grab the rabbit, but I got in front of her and took the animal out of the boy's hands.

"Now listen," I said as cool as possible. "I want a rabbit for my . . . er . . . little sister . . . and I need to know what kind of house it comes from. And the best way to find that out is to take some interest in the **owner**. So before I make a decision, I need to know a bit more about you."

---

to butt in – dazwischenplatzen;
gobsmacked – baff; unabashed – dreist;
bunny – Häschen; owner – Besitzer/Besitzerin

Flippi rolled her eyes.

"Do you like animals?" Max came back into the conversation.

"Of course I do. I'm a real animal lover. I always **judge** people according to their pets. Show me your pet and I'll tell you who you are ..." I **rambled on**.

But Flippi interrupted me again. "Just give me my bunny, will you?!" she grumbled, trying to get hold of the rabbit.

I held it above my head.

"He doesn't like that," said Moritz, pointing to Blacky. The rabbit was **wriggling around** in my hand. "Besides, he's not a bunny or a **hare**," he told Flippi.

"I'll decide that for myself," said Flippi. "And if I say it's a hamster with long ears, then it's a hamster with long ears."

I took the animal down from above my head and Flippi tried to grab it again. I didn't want a fight so I just let her have it.

"The bunny is sweet. We'll take it," Flippi decided and she was about to **head off** to the front door.

That wasn't on. First I had to win Max's **confidence** and arrange to meet him.

---

to judge – beurteilen;
to ramble on – weiterschwafeln;
to wriggle around – herumzappeln;
hare – Hase; to head off – ansteuern;
confidence – Vertrauen

I grabbed Flippi by the collar. "Not so fast!" I cried, racking my brains **feverishly**.

Flippi broke free and was already at the cellar door. I was **running out of time**. I started to panic.

"Hey," I said to Max as if I'd come up with the idea **entirely** spontaneously, "what about meeting up tomorrow afternoon?"

Max shrugged his shoulders.

"At three o'clock? At the **fountain** in the shopping centre?" I suggested.

Max eventually responded. "Shall I bring the rabbit with me?"

"What rabbit?"

He pointed at Flippi's hands.

"Oh, yes, of course! Definitely!" I cried straightaway.

"No," **announced** Flippi. "I'm taking it with me now."

"No," I said with all the authority I could muster. "We'll ... we have to get things ready first ... We'll do that tomorrow."

Flippi was **livid**. I took advantage of the moment of shock and **snatched** the rabbit out of her hands. Then I gave it back to Max.

---

feverish – fieberhaft;
to run out of time – keine Zeit mehr haben;
entirely – total; fountain – Brunnen;
to announce – bekannt geben;
livid – wütend;
to snatch – schnappen

“Max will bring it with him tomorrow,” I told Flippi like a primary school teacher.

I had to have some reason to meet up with him again.

Flippi stuck her tongue out.

We walked home next to each other in silence.

Flippi kept **glancing at** me out of the corner of her eye. In the end, she broke the silence. “So, you can do my Maths homework for a week.”

“Why should I do that?” I asked with a **mocking** laughing.

“Because you **tricked** me! You were after the boy, not the rabbit. You’re a walking embarrassment,” said Flippi decisively.

“I beg your pardon?!” I cried in outrage.

Flippi just shook her head. “Sometimes I really wonder if we’re **related**.”

“We’re not,” I spat back at her. “We got you out of the **animal home**.”

“And you *belong* in one,” **countered** Flippi. “Besides, I’m going to tell Mummy everything.”

I **stopped in my tracks**, furious. “That’s pure **blackmail**!”

---

to glance at – einen Blick werfen auf;
mocking – höhnisch; to trick sb – jmdn. reinlegen;
to be related – verwandt sein;
animal home – Tierheim; to counter – kontern;
to stop in one’s tracks – plötzlich stehen bleiben;
blackmail – Erpressung

Flippi shook her head. “What makes you say that? I’m giving you a choice.”

I thought about it for a second and decided that I’d rather not take the risk of having another mother-daughter conversation with my mum. “**It’s a deal**, you wally. I’ll do it.”

“Smart decision!” grinned Flippi.

It really should be Lucilla’s job to do Flippi’s homework. After all, I was doing all this just for her. All I had to do now was make sure that Lucilla came with me the next day.

Friday 19th January

When I came home from school, the phone was once again ringing like crazy. It’s obviously a busy business, the animal **trade**.

But there was little of interest amongst the calls apart from a boy who was looking for someone to **go walkies** with his dog **now and again**. That **sounded familiar**. I gratefully **turned down** the offer straightaway.

I’d fallen for a charlatan like that once before. I

It’s a deal. – Abgemacht.;
trade – Handel; to go walkies – Gassi gehen;
now and again – ab und zu;
to sound familiar – bekannt vorkommen;
to turn down – ablehnen

ended up not only taking his dog for a walk, I even **dyed** my hair blond for him. Flippi **made disparaging remarks** back then for weeks, saying, "Love makes people go soft in the head."

My mum changed the **phrase** slightly to "Love makes people go blond in the head," but that didn't help much either. The whole thing was really embarrassing. The only good thing about it was that I **got to know** Sven back then.

Then there was another call from the guy who wanted to sell me a one-eyed frog. He seriously tried to tell me all the advantages of a **limping goanna**. Like the fact that he would never run away. At least not far. What does the guy think I'm doing here? Setting up a sanatorium for reptiles?

When he said that his mother was giving him **aggro** about his pets and that he'd throw in a **tame rat** for free if I took the goanna, **my ears pricked up**. Stressed mothers suggest there's a teenager in the house. So I asked him to come to the fountain.

Two boys – a **measly return** for such a nice advertisement.

---

to dye – färben; to make disparaging remarks – lästern;
phrase – Spruch;
to get to know sb – jmdn. kennenlernen;
to limp – hinken; goanna – Waran;
aggro – Ärger; tame rat – zahme Ratte;
to prick up one's ears – hellhörig werden;
measly return – mickriger Gewinn

Friday evening 19th January

It was a complete **flop**. Actually, flop is an **understatement**.

Hardly surprising.

I was waiting in front of the fountain in the shopping centre with Lucilla. I was really nervous. The whole time I was trying to work out how I would explain the guys and animals to her, but I couldn't think of anything.

So I didn't say anything. Just: "You know, Lucilla, sometimes you just have to hang around ... then you might just meet the man of your dreams."

I thought that would prepare the ground for what was to come.

Lucilla nodded. "Yes, that's how it was with Niko."

"Forget about Niko," I snarled.

"Never!" replied Lucilla.

Come on, girl! How is Lucilla meant to fall in love with another boy if she keeps thinking about Niko? But I didn't want to start another **row** with her.

When Max finally turned up, Lucilla squealed in my ear, "Oh, how sweet!"

For me that meant all my problems were solved. I waved over to Max **effusively**. Then I introduced him to Lucilla. It was a bit embarrassing because Lucilla kept saying, "How sweet! I think he's really cute!"

---

flop – Pleite; understatement – Untertreibung;
row – Streit; effusive – überschwänglich

I mean, a bit of enthusiasm is okay, but you don't have to **overdo** it. Never show a boy you like him straightaway.

But it was all just a misunderstanding. I only realized this when Lucilla reached over to Max and **stroked** his hand. Well, not his hand exactly. The rabbit in his hands. At least she found the bunny good. It's a start.

But that was all she liked. All of a sudden, a guy tapped Lucilla on the shoulder and asked, "Hey, are you Jojo?"

Lucilla spun around and almost jumped out of her skin. Standing in front of her was a kind of punk with a goanna under his arm. He had a friend with him carrying a snake, dressed in **leather**. That is, the friend was dressed in leather, not the snake – although to be fair on the snake, it was also wearing leather. Of the snakeskin **variety**.

That brings us up to three candidates now, I thought, trying to be optimistic.

Lucilla looked shocked and **stammered** a reply. "N-no".

I was just about to reveal my identity when Lucilla pointed at me and said, "And that's not Jojo either."

I was surprised by her presence of mind in the situation. Not usually her **style**.

---

to overdo – übertreiben;
to stroke – streicheln;
leather – Leder; variety – Variation;
to stammer – stammeln; style – Art

“I said the girl wasn’t right in the head!” snarled the snake boy to his goanna friend. Then he smiled **longingly** at Max’s rabbit, **patted** his snake on the head and mumbled, “Looks like a tasty breakfast, huh, Sammy?”

Sammy’s forked tongue shot out of his mouth and Max turned pale.

Lucilla pulled my **sleeve**. “Come on, let’s get out of here,” she whispered

I let her pull me away, then I remembered poor Max who was still standing there, completely **motionless**, looking **spellbound** at the snake.

I ran back. “Come on, Max, come with us,” I said.

At the same time the goanna boy grabbed my sleeve. “Wait a second,” he said. “You’re Jojo. I recognize your voice.”

I went pale, tearing my eyes open in fear.

He put the goanna on the floor and pressed the **lead** into my hand. The lead went all the way to the goanna’s neck, just like a dog’s.

The guy patted the goanna on the head again. “He’s called ‘Killer’,” he told me. “You can call him something else if you want. It won’t make any difference. He won’t listen to you anyway.” Then the guy turned around and **trudged** off with his friend.

---

longing – begehrlich;
to pat – tätscheln; sleeve – Ärmel;
motionless – bewegungslos;
spellbound – wie verzaubert;
lead – Leine; to trudge – schlurfen

"Wait," I called after him in panic, "stop … I can't … you can't …"

"Look, I already told somebody else they could have the rat, but if you really want him, you can have him as well." He pulled a rat out of the inside pocket of his coat and was about to come back over to me.

"No!" I yelled in panic. "It's okay. No rat. The goanna's just fine."

The guy nodded and headed off. I just stood there with Killer on the lead, looking gobsmacked at Max.

"I've never met anyone who loves animals as much as you," he said.

I tried to smile. "Well, that's me! Just crazy about them."

"You wanted to take me for an ice cream!" Lucilla called from a **distance**.

I nodded robotically and set off after her.

I **plodded** along behind Lucilla, Max was behind me. Killer limped behind all three of us. Heading **mindlessly** for the ice-cream shop.

In front of the ice-cream shop I gave Max the lead and Lucilla and I got three ice creams to take away.

I tried not to think about the limping goanna for a minute and when we were alone, I asked Lucilla, "And? What do you think of him?"

---

distance – Entfernung;
to plod – trotten; mindless – wie betäubt

"Really sweet. I've always wanted one like that. But my mum won't let me."

"You mean the rabbit, right?" I guessed.

"Of course. What else would I be talking about?"

"The boy? I mean, he's really nice!"

"But he's a head smaller than me and ..." Lucilla suddenly looked at me with wide-open eyes, "... You're not trying to **set me up with** him, are you?!"

"Oh, get real! What makes you think that?" I said, waving my hand dismissively.

But for some reason Lucilla was sceptical. "Where did you meet him?"

That was one of the questions I hadn't found an answer for yet. "Er ... Flippi. I met him with Flippi." That wasn't a lie, was it?

"He's really nice," I tried again.

"But he's really small," ascertained Lucilla.

"He's 14 years old!"

"Are you serious? He looks about twelve."

"I **swear**, he's 14!" I repeated energetically.

Lucilla shrugged her shoulders. "Yeah, but boys who hang around shopping centres in the afternoon with a rabbit in their arms are just ..." **pondered** Lucilla, "... well, you know."

I groaned. My **patience** was at its end. "So, you don't like him then?" I asked somewhat curtly.

---

to set sb up with – jmdn. verkuppeln mit;
to swear – schwören; to ponder – nachdenken;
patience – Geduld

“No. I already said!” Lucilla was starting to get a bit **irritable** as well. Then she happened to look at the goanna which Max was holding on the lead. She gave me a nudge. “Look what he keeps on the lead,” she said **appalled**. “What is that?”

“That’s a goanna,” I said, annoyed. I went over to Max, took the lead out of his hand and added crossly, “*My* goanna. His name’s Killer and don’t say anything about his **disability**!”

Lucilla didn’t say a word. She’d just spotted Carla. She was standing in front of the pizzeria with Marc and a few other boys.

“Hey!” called Lucilla. “Hi, Carla!”

Carla of all people! She was the last person I wanted to see me standing next to a boy a head smaller than me with a rabbit in his arms and a goanna on the lead. Carla’s nasty comments would know no end.

“Not so loud,” I tried to hold Lucilla back. “**Otherwise** she might hear you!”

Lucilla looked at me confused. “She’s meant to hear me. That’s why I called her name.” She **took a deep breath** to call Carla’s name again.

“No, wait,” I stopped her. “Why don’t you just go over to her and surprise her?”

“Good idea.” Lucilla shrugged her shoulders and set off. When she realized I wasn’t coming with her,

---

irritable – gereizt; appalled – entsetzt;
disability – Behinderung; otherwise – sonst;
to take a deep breath – tief Luft holen

she stopped in her tracks. "What's the matter? Aren't you coming with me?"

I shook my head. "No. Max can come with you," I suggested quickly, smiling at Max **invitingly**. I wasn't going to give up that easily.

Then Max **stabbed me in the back**. "No," he said. "I'd rather not."

That didn't bother Lucilla. She headed off towards Carla.

Max turned to me and gave me a big smile. "And what are we going to do now?"

With an eye on Carla, I tried to disappear as **discreetly** as possible. I took my goanna under my arm. "We're going home," I said to Max without thinking.

"Great," replied Max and he started to follow me home.

I was completely **lost in thought**. I was racking my brains to work out why my plan had **backfired** and what had happened to get me this goanna under my arm. I only noticed that Max was **obediently** following me by the time I was standing in front of my front door.

I **gave a** slight **start** and said, "Huh? What are you doing here?"

---

inviting – einladend;
to stab sb in the back – jmdm. in den Rücken fallen;
discreet – diskret;
to be lost in thought – in Gedanken versunken sein;
to backfire – fehlschlagen; obedient – gehorsam;
to give a start – zusammenzucken

"You said we were going home."

"Yeah, but I was talking about me and ..." For some reason I couldn't finish my sentence. It was just the way he was standing there opposite me with his big eyes and a rabbit in his arms.

Oh boy, what had I gone and **got myself into** now?

I looked at Max and thought for a second.

All of a sudden, Max started to get **chatty**. "That was a really nice afternoon. Perhaps we could meet up some time and do it again?"

Sure thing. It was exactly what I'd always imagined as a perfect afternoon. A guy with a rabbit, a limping goanna, a huge snake, two punks in leather, Lucilla and then running away from Carla.

What was I supposed to say to Max?!

I **happened to** glance along the street and immediately broke into a panic: Sven was **strolling** along the road in my direction. I was **overcome** by a guilty feeling. I'd completely forgotten that he wanted to come around.

Sven came up to me and was about to kiss me when I quickly **bent over** and pretended to do something to my shoe. I wanted to avoid kissing

---

to get oneself into sth – sich etwas einbrocken;
chatty – gesprächig;
to happen to do sth – zufällig etwas tun;
to stroll – schlendern;
to be overcome – überwältigt sein;
to bend over – sich vorbeugen

Sven in front of Max. For some reason I found it embarrassing.

"Have you lost something?" Sven asked.

"No, I just have to **do up** my shoe."

"But your boots don't have any **shoelaces**," Sven pointed out to me **by the by**. Then he spotted the goanna. "I don't want to **disconcert** you, Jojo, but you've got a reptile on the end of the lead!" he said, pointing at Killer.

"That's a goanna. He limps."

"Oh, well that explains everything," replied Sven, nodding.

"Jojo is very **fond of** animals," **chipped in** Max.

It was only then that Sven noticed Max. I held my breath for a second because I had no idea how I was going to explain who Max was.

But Sven found an **explanation** for himself. "Hi," he said to Max in a friendly manner. Then he looked at the rabbit and asked, "Is Flippi **swapping** to rabbits?"

I didn't say anything in the hope that the conversation would take a good **turn** and leave me **in the clear**.

---

to do up – *hier:* binden;
shoelaces – Schnürsenkel;
by the by – leichthin; to disconcert – beunruhigen;
to be fond of sth – etwas gern mögen;
to chip in – dazwischenreden;
explanation – Erklärung;
to swap – tauschen, *hier:* umsteigen auf;
turn – Wendung; in the clear – aus allem heraus

Max didn't say anything either.

"Or is the rabbit the goanna's dinner?" prompted Sven.

"Of course not," I said and decided to go along with Sven's first explanation, "Max is just bringing around a rabbit for Flippi."

My guilty conscience was **niggling** away at me. No idea why.

"So, thanks a lot," I said to Max, taking the rabbit out of his hands.

I was just about to go into my house with Sven when Max **hesitantly** called after me. "Er, Jojo ... "

I turned around with a start. What was it now?

"Five euros," he stammered. "The rabbit costs five euros."

"Oh," I cried in surprise. For some reason it just hadn't **occurred to** me that animals actually cost money. After all, Killer hadn't cost me a penny. "Er, of course ... " Now I was stuttering, too.

Max noticed that I was embarrassed. "If you haven't got any money left then I'll give it to you as a present. After all, you paid for my ice cream."

"No, it's okay," I said quickly, turning red, "I'll pay for it."

But Max had already **made up his mind**. "We can sort that out another time. I'll give you a call." Then he left.

---

to niggle – nagen;
hesitant – zögerlich; to occur to sb – jmdm. einfallen;
to make up one's mind – sich entscheiden

Sven looked at me with wide-open eyes. “Is there something I need to know?”

I shook my head. “Nothing apart from the fact that I’m a **blithering idiot**.”

“I know that already,” said Sven **drily**, holding open the door for me.

I felt bad.

Sven obviously spotted this because he took me in his arms. “What have you been up to now?” he asked with a grin.

I just said, “Nothing at all!” And I wished it were true.

And there was something else giving me a major **headache**: What do goannas eat?

Saturday 20th January

My whole plan with the personal ad had led to nothing. Apart from two pets. Flippi immediately **impounded** one of them, the rabbit, and gave me her Maths homework to do.

The thing that really bothers me is that I still haven’t found out what a goanna eats.

Yesterday I took everything that looked like food

---

blithering idiot – Vollidiot;
dry – trocken;
headache – Kopfschmerzen;
to impound – beschlagnahmen

out of the fridge and brought it to my room – and that was a lot, because most of the time our food looks like something for **cold-blooded animals**. But Killer didn't eat anything.

I was sitting in the corner of my room because I was scared of Killer. Killer sat in the opposite corner.

He was living in my room. I couldn't even **fob him off on** Flippi because she was convinced that snails were his favourite food.

I don't want a goanna. Not even if he limps. To be honest, it's Lucilla's goanna. She should take him!

But she didn't want to. She wasn't **willing** to accept that she had anything to do with it either, and I didn't want to explain everything right down to the last detail.

Then Flippi came along and asked me to look after her "bunny" while she ran through the snails' training programme. Blacky always looked at her snails hungrily when they were doing their exercises.

Okay, so I took Blacky into my room as well. Killer, however, looked at the rabbit so **greedily** that I didn't dare let him onto the floor.

I just kept Blacky tucked under my arm, making

---

cold-blooded animal – Kaltblüter;
to fob sth off on sb – jmdm. etwas aufschwatzen;
willing – bereit;
greedy – gierig

sure there were always a few metres between me, Killer and Blacky. Not the easiest **task** in a kid's room by the way.

In the end, I was so **at a loss** that I called Sven and asked him to come around so that I could **pour out my heart** to him.

But Sven wasn't in a position to comfort me.

In fact, he just **laughed his head off**. As soon as he had calmed himself down a bit, he started laughing again. I just sat next to him and waited for him to stop, but in the end, I lost my patience.

"Well, I'm glad you find all this so amusing!" I snapped at him.

No reaction.

"Why don't you just tell me what I should do?" I said.

"No sudden **movements**," said Sven, pretending to be scared of Killer and trying not to laugh.

"No, tell me what I should do about Lucilla!" I **whinged**.

Sven tried to calm himself down and then said frankly, "I told you ages ago: talk to her."

"Pff," was all I could say, "how **uninspired**."

---

task – Aufgabe;
to be at a loss – nicht mehr weiterwissen;
to pour out one's heart – sein Herz ausschütten;
to laugh one's head off – sich totlachen;
movement – Bewegung;
to whinge – meckern;
uninspired – einfallslos

"And **give** the strange rescue missions **a break**. They don't do anything." Then he looked at Blacky and Killer and grinned. "Well, actually, maybe they do. They get you a rabbit and a goanna."

I decided not to comment.

"What does your mum say about all this?" asked Sven.

"Nothing."

"She doesn't know?" said Sven, guessing correctly.

Right **on cue** my mum came into my room. "Jojo, I just wanted to remind you that I'm going out tonight. You said you would look after Flippi."

Everything would have gone smoothly if I hadn't looked so nervously at my animals.

Mum noticed my reaction and posed the **unpleasant** question, "What's going on here?"

"They belong to Sven," I said like a shot.

Sven looked at me. Mum looked at me.

I have no problem **maintaining eye contact** with my mum when she stares at me, but not with Sven.

"They're mine," I mumbled. "But it was an accident," I added quickly.

"It's really not her fault." Sven **came to my rescue**. "I mean, considering Jojo is Jojo," he grinned.

---

to give sth a break – mit etwas pausieren;
on cue – aufs Stichwort;
unpleasant – unangenehm;
to maintain eye contact – einem Blick standhalten;
to come to sb's rescue – jmdm. zu Hilfe kommen

My mum thinks very highly of Sven, so she accepted this explanation. "Okay, fine. I won't even ask where the animals come from, but they have no place in this house. I'm ..."

The doorbell rang.

"Oh, that'll be Oskar," cried my mum and ran to the door.

Obviously, my mother had nothing better to do than tell Oskar everything about my zoo **within** the first two and a half seconds of him coming into our house. A few seconds after she was finished, she **dragged** him into my room.

"See, here ..." she said, waving her hands wildly at the animals. "A rabbit and a **weird lizard**."

Oskar laughed. "Jojo's always good for a surprise."

"That's not funny," Mum **scolded** him.

"And what are you going to do now?" Oskar asked me.

"I have to get rid of them somehow. Especially the goanna," I grumbled full of **regret**. "The question is: how?"

"You could put an advertisement in the paper," said Sven with a grin.

Sven must be out of his mind! What was the big idea?!

---

within – innerhalb;
to drag – schleppen;
weird – merkwürdig; lizard – Echse;
to scold – ausschimpfen; regret – Bedauern

“I want these animals out of my flat,” complained my mother, annoyed by the fact that Oskar found the situation funny. “Today!”

Oskar seemed to take the **responsibility** onto himself. All of a sudden he said, “I’ve always wanted a goanna.”

“He limps,” I warned him cautiously.

“I’ve always wanted a limping goanna,” Oskar corrected himself. “And every good home needs a rabbit,” he added, looking at my mum **beseechingly**.

“Oh, yes!” I cried immediately. “He’s really sweet! I always wanted a rabbit. Please, Mum!”

“And I always wanted a daughter with a head on her shoulders,” replied my mum **brusquely**.

That really made me angry. “You can **count yourself lucky** I don’t have a rat as well,” I informed my mother curtly. “I just about managed to get out of that.”

My mother gasped. “*I* can count myself lucky?! My dear Josefine, now you just listen to me: you’re ... ”

Oskar put his hand on Mum’s shoulder to calm her down. “Don’t get worked up, Isolde. I’ll take the animals. The rabbit, too.”

Mum looked at Oskar lovingly. “You’ll take the whole menagerie to your place?!”

---

responsibility – Verantwortung;
beseeching – flehentlich; brusque – schroff;
to count oneself lucky – von Glück reden können

"With or without the children?" asked Oskar.

"The children can stay here. I need them to scream at. Just take the animals, will you."

"If it helps," said Oskar **gently**.

Mum relaxed. "Thanks," she whispered.

"I'm all alone in my big house anyway," added Oskar **suggestively**.

It was an **insinuation** which Mum understood perfectly well. Her **lips** suddenly **tightened**. Oskar has not only been wanting to marry my mum for years, he wants us to move in with him.

But Oskar always picks the wrong moment to make such comments. It's purely instinctive and as **regular as clockwork**. Hard to believe, really.

Before my mum started to have a row with Oskar, I quickly threw my arms around his neck and thanked him effusively.

I was really relieved. Of two pets in fact.

Mum pulled her bittersweet face and just said, "But Jojo can pay for the pet food from her pocket money."

"Of course," said Oskar, winking at me **furtively**.

"Couldn't you take Flippi as well?" I asked Oskar quietly.

---

gentle – sanft;
suggestive – andeutend;
insinuation – Anspielung;
sb's lips tighten – jmd. kneift die Lippen zusammen;
regular as clockwork – pünktlich wie ein Uhrwerk;
furtive – heimlich

“Any time,” he whispered back, “if you can **smuggle** her past your mum.”

Oskar is just great. One day I’ll have to make sure he has his **wedding**. This man was made for our family.

Sunday 21st January

Sometimes life is good to me.

And how sweet it can be! Lucilla called and asked if it would be okay if she didn’t go out with me and Sven today. She’d decided she was going to call Niko and she needed all her energy for that.

I **generously** said it would be fine if she left us alone and could hardly wait to tell Sven the good news.

Sven was surprisingly **reserved** in his reaction, but he didn’t want to tell me why.

Flippi **blew her top** yesterday when she found out that Mum had moved out the new pets. “Then I’m going to move in with Oskar!” she swore and started packing her things.

---

to smuggle – schmuggeln;
wedding – Hochzeit;
generous – großzügig;
reserved – zurückhaltend;
to blow one’s top – einen Tobsuchtsanfall bekommen

I **gave her a hand**, which only got me into trouble with my mum. I can't do anything right for her either. I was just trying to be nice.

Mum then called Oskar in despair. He came around straightaway and solved the problem.

"That's great, Flippi," he said. "It's great that you're moving in with me."

Mum was just about to protest, but Oskar held up his hand. "You asked me to come here and sort this out," he said. "So let me do it." Then he turned back to Flippi. "It's high time that someone moved in with me. Then I can finally play Halma with someone. And you can help me sort out my **stamp collection,** too!"

"Forget it," said Flippi, continuing to pack.

"Oh well, never mind. At least we can sort out our socks **according to** their colour. And put the **jars of spices** in alphabetical order. That'll be fun!" said Oskar, handing Flippi a couple of towels to pack.

Flippi looked at Oskar sceptically.

"Doesn't **take your fancy**?" asked Oskar **amiably**. "Oh well, it's not the end of the world. There are plenty of other exciting things we can do. Like cleaning the **tiles** in the bathroom. Or **weeding** the garden. Oh, we'll have so much fun!"

---

to give sb a hand – jmdm. helfen;
stamp collection – Briefmarkensammlung;
according to – nach; jar of spices – Gewürzdose;
to take sb's fancy – jmdm. gefallen; amiable – freundlich;
tile – Kachel; to weed – Unkraut jäten

"Listen, Oskar," said Flippi, "I don't have time for things like that. After all, I go to school!"

"Oh, forget about school!" cried Oskar, waving his hand dismissively. "Nobody needs school. I can teach you how to **peel** potatoes and use a washing machine. That's all you need to know."

"But I want to go to school," said Flippi **stubbornly**.

"Alright then," **conceded** Oskar while handing Flippi a pile of pullovers. "Hey!" he added cheerfully. "Then we can do your Maths homework together. Multiplication tables. We can pass the time asking each other difficult mathematical problems, yeah?"

"No," replied Flippi **emphatically**.

Oskar **frowned**. "Why do you want to move in to my place if you don't want to do anything with me?"

"I'm coming because of my animals!"

"Oh, right. That's good. Because they're really dirty and they're a lot of work. They almost take up my entire day. Cleaning the **cages**, preparing food. I'm glad that will be over when you come. I hardly have time for anything else at the moment. I'm just looking after animals from morning till night."

---

to peel – schälen;
stubborn – starrköpfig;
to concede – nachgeben;
emphatic – nachdrücklich;
to frown – die Stirn runzeln;
cage – Käfig

"I thought you went to work?" Flippi asked suspiciously.

Oskar sighed. "Not since I've had the animals. No time, you see."

"Aha? And what are you living off?"

"That's a problem. But when you move into my place we can live off your pocket money."

"No way."

"Alright. Then I'll go back to work and you look after the house."

"You know what, Oskar, I think you're going to have to solve your problems on your own. Forget about me," said Flippi, unpacking her things. As she went past Mum, she whispered, "Don't marry him. He can hardly **stand on his own two feet**."

Sunday evening 21st January

Can you believe that??! Why is the whole world against me?

It all started really well. I was over the moon.

The cinema with Sven. Alone. All by ourselves. Just me and Sven. And a rabbit. Seriously. Sven came with a rabbit.

Sven is soooo sweet.

When he picked me up, he really did have a

---

to stand on one's own two feet – selbstständig sein

bunny in his arms, but it was of the **fluffy** variety, not a real one, of course. Really sweet.

"What did I do to deserve this?"

Sven gave me a slightly bittersweet smile. "First of all, yesterday you said you wanted a rabbit."

"Aha. And secondly?"

"Do you really want to know?" he asked with an **agonized** expression on his face.

"Of course I do!" I insisted.

Sven gave a sigh. "Secondly, it's a **peace offering**."

"A peace offering? But we're not even at **war**."

Sven sighed again. "Not yet."

I was really taken aback. "Not yet? What's that meant to mean? Do you want to start an argument with me?"

Sven **denied** this emphatically. "Of course not. I would never start an argument with you! Ever!"

"So who's meant to start the argument?"

"You!"

I laughed out loud. "You must be out of your mind, Sven! I'm not going to start a row with you!"

"Yes, you are," said Sven with a nod of his head.

I was starting to get nervous. "Why do you think I'm going to start an argument with you? And when?"

"When we get to the cinema and you meet Andreas."

---

fluffy – kuschelig; agonized – gequält;
peace offering – Friedensangebot;
war – Krieg; to deny – verleugnen, *hier:* verneinen

"Andreas?"

"Yeah. A new guy in our class. He moved here recently. My mum met his mother and she talked me into meeting up with him. There was nothing I could do. I promised her I'd keep an eye on him until he makes some friends!" Sven looked really depressed.

I looked at Sven **blankly**.

We'd only just got rid of Lucilla and we still weren't alone together. Well, marvellous.

"Are you angry?" asked Sven apologetically.

I thought about this for a second, but then I found it all incredibly funny.

I started to laugh and couldn't stop. I laughed my head off.

"Man, if I'd have known it would make you this happy, I'd have invited a few more boys from my class."

I was still laughing.

Sven grabbed the rabbit. "Can I have the rabbit back if there's no war?"

I laughed, held tightly onto the rabbit and gave Sven a hug.

Sven looked at me lovingly. "You really aren't angry about Andreas?"

I shook my head. "**Not in the slightest**. At least then you can see what it's like for me. Andreas is your Lucilla."

---

blank – ausdruckslos;
not in the slightest – nicht die Bohne

Sven kissed me.

"Come on, let's take a look at the **lad**," I said. "Maybe he's not all that bad."

"There's just one **favour** I have to ask you."

"What?"

"Please don't kiss him."

"What's that supposed to mean? What makes you think I would do something like that?"

Sven grinned. Then I remembered Marc and turned red.

But Andreas was awful. He spoke non-stop and was a real **know-all**. He had an opinion about everything. Even during the film!

Not a scene passed by without his quiet commentary. "Badly **dubbed**," he said every two minutes. "You can see it if you watch their lips closely," he explained to me. "It's probably badly translated as well and they ruined the **punchline**."

Did I mention that he was sitting between us? Not bad, huh? Let's just say, I was pretty **cheesed off**.

After the cinema Andreas suggested we go for a pizza. "Then we can discuss the film in detail."

"What for?" I asked, **dumbfounded**.

---

lad – Knabe;
favour – Gefallen;
know-all – Besserwisser;
dubbed – synchronisiert;
punchline – Pointe;
cheesed off – verärgert; dumbfounded – verblüfft

"Oh, come on," he told me off. "One doesn't go to the cinema to be amused."

"Oh really? Why does 'one' go to the cinema then?"

"To be alone with your girlfriend?" suggested Sven innocently.

"To talk about the film!" said Andreas, ignoring Sven's **allusion**.

"But you did that during the film," I said cheekily.

"Yes, but only **superficially**. I didn't want to talk the whole time. Otherwise it's impossible to watch the film **properly**."

Thanks to Andreas' **waffle** I hadn't been able to watch the film properly anyway.

"For example," continued Andreas, "I noticed that the **editing** gave the **plot** a completely different structure."

"Quite," said Sven, agreeing with Andreas immediately. "And the **lighting** at the beginning ... it was really very dark!"

Andreas seemed puzzled. "It was meant to be night," he told Sven. He obviously didn't **grasp** Sven's sense of humour.

---

allusion – Andeutung;
superficial – oberflächlich;
proper – richtig; waffle – Geschwätz;
editing – Schnitt; plot – Handlung;
lighting – Beleuchtung;
to grasp – verstehen

"Oh," said Sven, "then that was really clever with the darkness and stuff."

Andreas **faltered** slightly but didn't let himself be **deterred**. He continued his lecture as we walked to the pizzeria.

We had to listen to Andreas analyzing the film all the way through our meal.

I groaned while **chewing** my pizza. Andreas had **spoilt** the whole film for me with his detailed breakdown. But at least we've **done a good deed**, I thought.

However, at a certain point you do reach your limit. For me it was the point when Andreas made the following suggestion: "And tomorrow we can watch the original version in English. Then you'll see the difference."

I gave Sven a meaningful look and he understood me straightaway.

"I don't have any time tomorrow," said Sven like a shot.

"Why not?"

"My grandma is going to show me how to **knit** socks."

---

to falter – stocken;
to deter – abschrecken;
to chew – kauern;
to spoil – verderben;
to do a good deed – eine gute Tat vollbringen;
to knit – stricken

My **jaw dropped in amazement**. Since when did Sven **tell fibs**?

Sven saw the look of astonishment on my face. “I get it from you,” he whispered.

“Okay,” said Andreas, satisfied. Then he turned to me. “What about you? Are you coming?”

I jumped and started coughing. “No,” I said. “I want to learn to knit as well.”

Andreas thought about this for a second. “Actually, that’s not a bad idea. Good. Alright then. Tomorrow we can go to this knitting course with Sven’s grandma. But we should go about it **methodically**. First of all we spin our own **wool**, then we can knit it.”

I looked at Sven in disbelief. Sven looked back at me in equal disbelief.

“When shall we meet? I’m free after 4 o’clock,” Andreas let us know.

I was really interested to see how Sven got out of this. I leant back and waited.

“No,” said Sven very resolutely. “I’m going to my grandma alone. Time with her is **precious**. And I wanted to learn how to knit socks on my own.”

I was really annoyed that Sven was **excluding** me from his excuse.

---

sb’s jaw drops in amazement – jmdm. fällt vor Staunen der Unterkiefer herunter; to tell a fib – flunkern;
methodical – methodisch;
wool – Wolle; precious – wertvoll;
to exclude – ausschließen

Andreas looked at me. "Well, looks like it'll be just the two of us going to the cinema."

"Too much cinema is bad for the eyes. I'm staying home," I said decisively.

When I said that I wanted to go home, Andreas said, "We'll **accompany** you, of course. It's only to be expected of a gentleman."

I looked at him in horror. I'd hoped to be alone with Sven at last. I looked at Sven, horrified, but he just shrugged his shoulders slightly.

We then trudged home. The three of us. Great afternoon.

Sven called me later and apologized. Not that it was necessary. I had **sympathy** for his situation. I really did.

Sven was relieved. "And do you know what we're going to do tomorrow?" he said, back in a good mood.

"Yes," I cried, "we're going to the cinema!"

"Exactly," laughed Sven. "We can watch the film again, without Andreas' comments!"

"I hope we understand it then."

"If not then we can always watch it again."

"And again and again. Until we finally get it."

We laughed our heads off. It's a great thing when you have a **common enemy**. Brings people together.

---

to accompany – begleiten; sympathy – Mitleid;
common enemy – gemeinsamer Feind

Monday 22nd January

Lucilla was **on cloud nine** this morning in school.

I didn't even have to ask what was going on. She just threw her arms around my neck when she saw me and chirped, "He's sooo sweet! You won't believe it."

I was really happy for her.

"What happened?" I asked her. "Tell me!"

"You just won't believe it!" she cried again.

"You never know, maybe I will. Give me a chance and tell me what happened!"

"Oh, Jojo!" she **went into raptures** and fell silent.

I started to grow **impatient**.

"Guess!" she **beamed at** me.

Oh man, I hate playing the game when Lucilla tells me to 'guess' and I haven't even got a clue what it's about.

But if I didn't at least try to guess, I would never find out what had happened.

"Niko is taking the next **flight** to come and visit you," I said **listlessly**.

Lucilla looked at me annoyed. "You spoilsport!" she moaned.

I rolled my eyes. "I'm sorry, Lucilla. Then just tell me."

---

to be on cloud nine – im siebten Himmel schweben;
to go into raptures – ins Schwärmen geraten;
impatient – ungeduldig; to beam at sb – jmdn. anstrahlen;
flight – Flug; listless – lustlos

"No, I can't be bothered now."

"Why not?"

"Because the surprise is over!"

"What do you mean?" I cried impatiently.

Lucilla shrugged her shoulders, offended. "I wanted to surprise you. But you know already."

"What?!" I asked in astonishment. "You mean, he's really coming?"

"Yes," scowled Lucilla, now in a bad mood.

"That is unbelievable!" I cried. "He's coming to visit you?"

Lucilla shrugged her shoulders.

"Hey, that's terrific! He's actually getting into a plane and coming to visit you. I can't believe it."

"No," said Lucilla, bored. "Not a plane."

"What do you mean? Is he coming or isn't he?"

"He's coming by train." Lucilla was still offended.

"And why are you in such a bad mood?" I asked.

"Because you spoiled the surprise for me."

"But you told me to guess."

"Yes, but you didn't have to come up with the right answer. What made you think of that anyway?"

"It was a wild idea, the craziest thing I could think of."

"Tzz," said Lucilla and fell silent.

"How did it happen then?" I asked. "I mean, him deciding to visit you?"

Lucilla beamed. "I asked him."

"Really? Boy, that was **brave**."

---

brave – mutig

"Why?"

"Well, you know, if he'd said 'no', it would have been really embarrassing."

"Why?"

I fell silent, **dismayed**. Hadn't anyone ever told Lucilla that it's embarrassing to get turned down? Or wasn't it as embarrassing as I always thought? Whatever.

"When's he coming?"

"Next weekend. He's staying at Sven's place. They're having some **family do**."

"Oh, so he's coming ..." I wanted to say 'because of the family do', but I bit my tongue. That would have been a bit mean to Lucilla. Instead I said, "... for the whole weekend. That's great."

Lucilla beamed and nodded. Then she hummed and hawed, "But listen, there's a slight problem."

"What kind of problem?"

"Well, you know, you and Sven. I mean, don't get me wrong, I really like you both a lot, but ..."

"But what?" I asked suspiciously.

"Well, you know, when Niko's here ... could the two of you go out on your own?"

I looked at her **utterly flabbergasted**. "Sorry?"

Lucilla pulled an unhappy face. "I knew you'd be angry with me. Please try to understand! I just really want to be alone with Niko. I know you two have **got**

---

dismayed – betroffen; family do – Familienfeier;
utterly flabbergasted – total von den Socken;
to get used to sth – sich an etwas gewöhnen

used to going out with me all the time, but this time I'd rather be alone with my boyfriend. Don't be angry with me."

"No problem," I said really coolly. "I can understand that."

"Oh no, you are angry with me," whined Lucilla.

"No, I'm not."

"Yes, you are."

"Lucilla, I'm not angry with you, and that's that!"

This is just too much to swallow.

For weeks I try to tell her as diplomatically as possible that I would like to be alone with Sven, and then this Niko boy comes along and she says right to my face that she wants to be alone with her "boyfriend". Unbelievable!

Friday 26th January

Oskar called and wanted to talk to me.

"It's about Blacky. Are you sure he's **male**?"

"Yes."

"Hm, then give the newspaper a call. We've got a sensation on our hands: Blacky's had babies."

"Whaaat?" I cried.

"Four of them."

"You're joking?!"

"Come round and take a look for yourself!"

---

male – männlich

Flippi and I immediately **hit the road**.

Flippi was in a really bad mood. She still hadn't forgiven me for letting the new pets go without a fight.

"I could now be the proud owner of five rabbits," she grumbled on the way to Oskar's. "And you ruined it all!"

When we got to Oskar's, he was sitting between a **batch** of rabbits looking really rather **distressed**. He kept **heaving** these deep **sighs**.

It's a strange **phenomenon**: most adults who come into contact with me and Flippi tend to sigh **at regular intervals**.

Poor Oskar. I felt a bit sorry for him. I had the feeling he'd done the whole animal thing just because he was in love with Mum.

Love does strange things to people.

"Stop pulling a face like that!" Flippi had a go at him. "Put yourself in my position!"

Oskar looked confused. "Help me out here. What are you talking about?"

"You've got all the fun now! Five rabbits, man! They could all be mine if Jojo wasn't such a **scaredy-cat**!"

---

to hit the road – sich auf die Socken machen;
batch – Schwung; distressed – bekümmert;
to heave a sigh – einen Seufzer ausstoßen;
phenomenon – Phänomen;
at regular intervals – in regelmäßigen Abständen;
scaredy-cat – Angsthase

A **flicker of hope** flashed over Oskar's face. He picked up all the rabbits and gave them to Flippi. "Take them! They're all yours!"

I looked at him suspiciously. What was going on here? He knew Mum would **hit the roof** if Flippi came home with the rabbits.

Then I realized what was going on. "Stress with Mum?"

Oskar nodded.

"The usual?"

Oskar shrugged his shoulders. Oh dear! He'd gone and asked her to marry him again.

I shook my head. "You just don't learn!"

"But she told me herself I would be the perfect husband."

"But **not necessarily** for *her*!"

Oskar shook his head. "That's right. She didn't say anything about that."

"Well then, there you have it."

My mum would **sulk** for a few days and then, if Oskar played his cards right, she would forgive him and everything would **start all over** again.

"What are you going to do now?" I asked, sitting down on the sofa.

But before my **bottom** made contact, Oskar

---

flicker of hope – Hoffnungschimmer;
to hit the roof – an die Decke gehen;
not necessarily – nicht unbedingt;
to sulk – schmollen; to start all over – von Neuem anfangen;
bottom – Hintern

gasped and grabbed me, pulling me away from the sofa.

"What it is?" I asked in surprise.

"Killer," sighed Oskar. "The sofa is his **domain**. He won't have anybody else sitting on it."

Killer was indeed sitting **stock-still** in the corner, watching me.

"Rubbish," I said and cautiously leant over to him.

Killer turned his head to me **as quick as a flash** and made a sound that sounded like a mixture of hissing and **spitting**.

I jumped back and looked at Oskar, horrified.

He shrugged his shoulders. "You don't stand a chance. The sofa belongs to him."

"And where do you sit when you're watching TV or reading?"

"Oh, I bring over a chair from the kitchen," said Oskar meekly.

"How uncomfortable!"

"Well, actually, the kitchen chair is the best part of the deal. The thing with the **inflatable mattress** is much more annoying."

I looked at Oskar inquisitively.

"Killer has also taken over my bed," he mumbled

---

domain – Gebiet;
stock-still – bewegungslos;
as quick as a flash – blitzschnell;
to spit – fauchen;
inflatable mattress – Luftmatratze

sheepishly. "I have to sleep on an inflatable mattress."

"**For crying out loud**, Oskar, **that's not on**! You have to **assert yourself**. Show him who's boss."

Oskar shook his head. "No, I'd rather not. He might think it's because of … well, you know … "

"No, I don't know. Because of what?"

Oskar **lowered** his voice. "Because of his … er," Oskar took a step towards me and whispered, "… his … disability."

"Oh, Oskar," I cried, "**grow up**!"

Flippi went to the sofa and was just about to sit down.

Oskar and I shouted at her **in unison,** "No, Flippi!" We rushed over to the sofa to rescue her.

But the matter had already been **dealt with**. Killer hissed at Flippi, Flippi hissed even louder and more ominously back at Killer. Then she sat down on the sofa and Killer limped away.

Flippi looked at us. "What's the matter?" she asked as Killer disappeared.

"Nothing," said Oskar. "No big deal."

I still had my hand on my heart and breathed out in relief. That was **a close shave**. I groaned. "Just

---

For crying out loud! – Mensch!;
That's not on. – Das geht nicht.;
to assert oneself – sich durchsetzen;
to lower – senken; Grow up! – Werd erwachsen!;
in unison – einstimmig;
to deal with – sich kümmern um;
a close shave – knapp

imagine," I said to Oskar while looking at Flippi, "even fully-grown lizards who can put their opponents out of action with a **mere whip of their tail** run away from this child. And I have to spend time, **day in and day out** with her under the same roof."

Oskar nodded with understanding. "Do you need a cup of tea?" he asked **apprehensively**, knowing of my mum's habits.

"Yes," I mumbled.

While Oskar made me a cup of tea – with a teabag in hot water, he's a real **pro** – I brought the conversation back round to him and Mum.

"And what are you going to do about Mum now?"

"Oh, I'll just tell her that I've thought it through and nothing in the world would bring me to marry her. That will **make it up to** her."

I rolled my eyes.

Oskar looked at me in surprise. "That won't make it up to her?" he asked.

I shook my head. "Tell her you love her and you'll do anything she wants," I explained.

"And that works?"

I shrugged my shoulders. "That's what I always say when I have trouble with her. It works every time."

---

mere – nur;
whip of the tail – Schwanzschlag;
day in and day out – tagein, tagaus;
apprehensive – besorgt;
pro – Profi;
to make it up to sb – etwas bei jmdm. wiedergutmachen

We Isolde-**damaged**-people do have to **stick together**.

"So, listen up!" **rang out** Flippi's voice suddenly. She came into the kitchen and handed Oskar a piece of paper. "I've written down the feeding times and a **nutritional plan**. Please **stick to** it! Animals need regularity in their lives."

I looked at Oskar in astonishment, but he always manages to **keep a straight face** while talking to Flippi.

"Thanks a lot," he said politely.

As we were leaving, I noticed that Flippi had something in her jacket pocket. It was **bulging** strangely. After casting a glance into the room with the rabbits, I noticed that Blacky was sitting there with only two of her children. Oskar needed all his **persuasiveness** to get Flippi to leave the children with their mother.

After that we set off home.

"It's not the same thing!" moaned Flippi **out of the blue**. "Visiting animals is stupid. I want my own pet!"

---

damaged – geschädigt;
to stick together – zusammenhalten;
to ring out – ertönen; nutritional plan – Ernährungsplan;
to stick to sth – sich an etwas halten;
to keep a straight face – ernst bleiben;
to bulge – ausbeulen;
persuasiveness – Überredungskunst;
out of the blue – aus heiterem Himmel

"I did what I could. Now it's up to you."

"No. It was because of you in the first place that I had the animals, and it's your fault that I don't have them any more. So it's clearly up to you. You have to get me a new pet."

"Oh really? And how am I meant to do that?" I said, annoyed. "Shall I **magic** one **up** for you?"

Flippi stopped in her tracks and looked at me. "Magic ..." she murmured, lost in thought. Then she cried, "Where's my magic bear?"

I jumped. "No idea," I replied quickly.

As soon as we got home, I would look for the magic bear and hide him so that Flippi would never find him again. The magic bear is a small **cuddly toy** which **makes** wishes **come true**. At least Flippi is quite convinced that wishes come true when she's holding the bear. More or less. That is, less rather than more. Though something always happens, even if it's **rarely** something good.

She still had him a few weeks ago, but somehow he must have got taken off in her rubbish and she'd forgotten about him.

Until now.

Until stupid old me said the word "magic". A short **lapse of concentration** and once again I'm liv-

---

to magic up – hervorzaubern;
cuddly toy – Stofftier;
to make sth come true – etwas in Erfüllung gehen lassen;
rarely – selten;
lapse of concentration – Konzentrationsmangel

ing in danger. I decided to make sure the bear would never **turn up**.

As we continued our way home, I realized how desperate I must be to have **undertaken** something with Flippi. Like going to visit animals and stuff.

But everybody else had been too busy!

Even Sven.

Sven was spending a lot of time with Andreas, introducing him to as many people as possible in the hope of getting rid of him soon. And then we'd be together again at last.

Not surprisingly, he'd said I could join him when he went out with Andreas, but he might as well have asked me to catch **chickenpox**.

Friday evening 26th January

We'd only just got home when Flippi started searching through the whole house, looking for her magic bear. She didn't find him, though, thank God. She **swore** out loud a lot and accused me and Mum of stealing her bear.

I pretended to find the accusation deeply **offen-**

---

to turn up – auftauchen;
to undertake – unternehmen;
chickenpox – Windpocken;
to swear – *hier:* schimpfen; offensive – beleidigend

sive. In the end, I even helped Flippi to look. The fact that there was a perfectly logical explanation behind the disappearance was something I kept to myself. Sadly, my search also ended **empty-handed**: no bear.

But I preferred to keep it that way.

Lucilla called later on.

She'd been talking about nothing else but Niko for days. She spent all her free time in front of her wardrobe, trying to decide what to wear at the weekend.

I asked her if she wanted to meet up, but she said she didn't have any time. Still too much to do before Niko got there.

For crying out loud, what did she have to do? **Redecorate** her room? Knit a red **carpet** for Niko? She was really throwing herself into it.

"What do you think, Jojo?" she asks me at least 32 times a day on the phone. "Red or blue?"

"Red," I say, because I've learnt not to ask Lucilla too many questions.

"But I don't look good in red!"

"Okay, then blue."

"But red is the colour of love."

"What about pink?"

"Pink is good."

---

empty-handed – mit leeren Händen;
to redecorate – neu streichen;
carpet – Teppich

She hangs up and calls again ten minutes later. "I don't have anything in pink."

"Green?"

"I don't like green."

"Yellow!" I say decisively.

"Okay."

Next call. "I decided to go for blue. What do you think?"

"Great idea."

Once the **question** of colour has been **settled**, the whole thing starts again: **jumper** or blouse? Skirt or trousers? Boots or trainers? And then comes the question of style: romantic or cool? Classic or sporty? **Whacky** or elegant? Oh, and not forgetting the **hairdo**.

And each day she tells me exactly how long it is until Niko gets here.

"Three days to go."

"Two days to go."

"He's coming tomorrow."

"He's coming today! Oh my God, I'm so excited! I can't possibly go."

"Of course you're going!" I told her off. After all, I'd **put up with** her preparations all week. I wasn't doing this all for nothing.

---

to settle a question – eine Frage klären;
jumper – Pullover;
whacky – abgefahren;
hairdo – Frisur;
to put up with sth – etwas ertragen

"What if he doesn't like me?"

"He will like you!"

"It's been such a long time since we saw each other!"

"That doesn't matter."

"To be honest, I don't know him at all."

Oh really? What makes you say that all of a sudden?

"Lucilla, just go."

"I could say I'm ill!"

"No!" I cried in despair. "Please meet up with him!"

"Alright then. But it's **on your shoulders**!"

The whole thing has left me feeling completely **shattered**. I'll be so happy when it's all over and life can go back to normal.

And as soon as Niko's gone, I'm going to tell Lucilla that Sven and I also want to go out on our own sometimes. **Yes, siree**!

---

on your shoulders – auf deine Verantwortung;
shattered – erschöpft;
Yes, siree! – Jawohl!

"How could you?!" **sobbed** Lucilla into the telephone. She was **in a state**.

I had no idea what she was talking about. Had I chosen the wrong colour for her dress?

"What is it? How could I what?" I asked.

"Niiikooo!" cried Lucilla.

Niko?

"What happened?" I asked anxiously.

"How could you?!" repeated Lucilla.

The conversation wasn't **making** much **progress**. What had happened with Niko?

"What did he do?" I asked tentatively.

"He's not good looking, he's not funny, and he's not romantic – he's nothing!"

"Oh, and that's all my fault, is it?" I asked, annoyed.

"And on top of that he lives 300 kilometres away!" she said reproachfully.

Now I really was flabbergasted. What was Lucilla trying to say?

"How could you let it happen?!" she cried **indignantly**.

I was still speechless.

"How can you let me fall in love with a boy like

---

to sob – schluchzen;
to be in a state – mit den Nerven fertig sein;
to make progress – vorankommen, Fortschritte machen;
indignant – empört

that?!" sobbed Lucilla. "You know how romantic I am!"

"Drama," I snarled quietly. "So your date wasn't exactly a **hit** ..." I **determined** objectively. It was about time we got to the point here.

"It was a disaster! I didn't even recognize him at first!"

"Well, that's not surprising." I tried to remain objective. "You did meet him at a **masked ball**."

"That's right. He was my Prince Charming from the Orient. He looked so sweet!"

"Did you expect him to come in **scarlet pantaloons** again?"

"No, of course not," said Lucilla, but she was lying.

"And what have I done wrong?" I came back to her initial accusation.

"You should have told me that a **long distance** relationship like that would never work."

"Er ... Lucilla ... I did ..." No, I couldn't speak, I was just too **dumbstruck**.

"Oh, Jojo, you have no idea what it feels like **to be lovesick**!"

"What?" I cried indignantly. "I have no idea? I

---

hit – Erfolg;
to determine – feststellen;
masked ball – Maskenball;
scarlet pantaloons – scharlachrote Pluderhosen;
long distance – Fern-;
dumbstruck – verblüfft;
to be lovesick – Liebeskummer haben

invented lovesickness. I've been lovesick thousands of times! My lovesickness would fill books!"

Lucilla still wasn't convinced.

"I've even been double-lovesick! Remember Justus and Lukas?" I reminded her. "That's when I realized: lovesickness is worth it!"

"But it's not," sobbed Lucilla. "What did it do for you? You didn't get either of them! Because they don't live here."

"But I've got Sven now! And that's much better!!"

It didn't help much because Lucilla just **blubbered** even louder. "Exactly, you've got Sven! And who loves me?! I haven't got anybody."

"What's so terrible about Niko? Why have you **gone off** him all of a sudden?"

"Because of everything!"

We both fell silent.

After a while Lucilla broke the silence. "He's really silly!" she whined.

"He's got a girlfriend, right?" All of a sudden, I knew exactly what the problem was.

"Yes. He's got a girlfriend. That's what I meant: the distance drew us **apart**."

Well, **besides** the fact that the two were never together in the first place, that's what I said from the very start, right? But who cares? That wasn't going to help now.

---

to blubber – heulen;
to go off sb – jmdn. nicht mehr mögen;
apart – auseinander; besides – außer

"Are you still in love with him?"

"Of course not!" cried Lucilla indignantly. "I can't be in love with someone who's not in love with me."

Well, well. If it was always that easy.

"So everything's fine really," I said.

"No, nothing is fine. Now I don't have a boyfriend. All the girls have got a boyfriend apart from me," moaned Lucilla.

That was a slight **exaggeration**. Carla and I were the only girls from our class who had a boyfriend.

"And who loves me?" Lucilla whined on. "No one!"

I tried to reassure her. "Come on, Lucilla, you'll meet the right person one day!"

"Oh yeah? And how?" She started to cry.

"I'll help you! I'll find a boyfriend for you!"

That was a mistake. I knew it as soon as the words came out of my mouth. But it was too late. What's said is said. I couldn't take it back.

Lucilla immediately stopped crying. "That's sooo nice of you, Jojo!" she said. "Thank you. And do you know what? I was thinking: the best way for me to meet boys is always to go out with you and Sven."

I swallowed and sighed **under my breath**.

I hadn't quite **digested** this piece of news when

---

exaggeration – Übertreibung;
under one's breath – leise vor sich hin;
to digest – verdauen

Lucilla started to tell me off. "But I don't want you to kiss each other all the time when we're out!"

"Why not?"

"Because it always makes me think: And who's kissing me?"

"I'll must tell Sven," I mumbled feebly and hung up.

Sven!

Sven will just have to live with it. After all, it was **partly** his fault as well.

I gave him a call. "We've got a problem!" I groaned into the phone.

"And a very good morning to you, too!" said Sven as **deadpan** as ever.

"Stop trying to sidetrack me," I grumbled.

"Tell me what I'm meant to sidetrack you from and I'll give it my best," laughed Sven.

"It's about Lucilla," I started to explain. "We have to find a boyfriend for her."

"We do?" said Sven. "Why doesn't that come as a surprise?"

"No, seriously. It's official now. Lucilla has asked me to help her find a boyfriend. Do you know anyone who might be a possibility?"

And then we both had exactly the same idea: "Andreas!" we cried **telepathically**.

"Okay," laughed Sven.

---

partly – teilweise;
deadpan – trocken;
telepathic – telepathisch

"Great idea!"

"Invite him over. I'll bring Lucilla. But no cinema!"

"Of course not. I'm not stupid. We can go bowling."

"That's a deal."

I'd hardly hung up when the phone rang again. It was Lucilla.

"And?" she asked.

"What do you mean, 'and'?"

"Have you found someone for me already?"

"Er … well … actually … We only spoke five minutes ago!"

"So what? A lot can happen in five minutes?"

She was right there. Who knows that better than me?!

"Have you told Sven already?" asked Lucilla.

I wasn't sure what to say to that. The chances of giving the wrong answer were fifty-fifty. Did Lucilla want me to tell Sven or not?

I decided on "No".

"Oh? Why not?" said Lucilla in a sulk. "After all, it's all your fault."

"Oh, you mean *that*!" I said quickly. "Of course I spoke to Sven about that."

"So?"

"So what?"

"Well, what did he say?"

"Er … not a lot."

"What? Not a lot?" cried Lucilla and it sounded

like she was about to **burst into tears**. "That shows just how much he cares!"

I swallowed. **Consolation** and some comforting words were called for here. "Oh, he does care. He really does. Sven is really sorry. Honestly. He really didn't think you'd fall in love with him that badly."

"What?! I'm not in love with Sven at all! What makes him think that?!"

"No, I mean with Niko."

It would have been better not to have mentioned the name again. Lucilla started sobbing. "And what is your boyfriend going to do now?" she asked.

"He's going to organize another Niko for you, of course!" I said like a shot.

"No, not another Niko. I want someone different."

"Yeah, yeah, sure thing. The new Niko is called Andreas."

"That doesn't sound very cool."

He's not, I almost said.

"So what's he like?"

"Oh well, he's really … er …" – a real know-all wasn't exactly the best **selling point** – "really … clever."

"Seriously?" Lucilla stopped crying **on the spot**.

"Yes. In fact, why don't we meet up in an hour?"

"Okay. I'm on my way."

---

to burst into tears – in Tränen ausbrechen;
consolation – Trost; selling point – Verkaufsargument;
on the spot – auf der Stelle

Sunday evening 28th January

Lucilla didn't turn up that quickly in the end. I guess the what-shall-I-wear-question **held** her **up** once again.

There was no sign of Andreas either, so Sven and I went in, reserved a **bowling alley** and changed our shoes.

Still no sign of Andreas and Lucilla.

"Hey," said Sven all of a sudden. "If we're lucky, neither of them will turn up."

"Or they met in front of the door, fell in love **at first sight** and have **run off** together," I suggested.

"That's how it would be if the gods loved us," sighed Sven, giving me a kiss.

"And who's going to kiss me?" asked someone behind us.

It was Andreas. What a shame.

We sent him off to get some bowling shoes and kissed again.

"And who's going to kiss me?" came another voice. This time it was Lucilla.

"They're perfect for each other," said Sven, **rubbing his hands together** while Lucilla went over to get her shoes.

---

to hold up – aufhalten;
bowling alley – Bowlingbahn;
at first sight – auf den ersten Blick;
to run off – *hier:* durchbrennen;
to rub one's hands together – sich die Hände reiben

As the future couple came back with their new **footwear**, we introduced them to each other.

"Hello," said Andreas **formally** and with a clear **lack of interest**.

Lucilla didn't even giggle. That was a bad sign.

We started bowling. **To be precise**, we were about to start bowling, but first of all we had to listen to one of Andreas' lectures about the **ins and outs** of bowling.

Lucilla had the nerve to interrupt Andreas' lecture and even **contradict** him. A long discussion **developed** between them.

Sven and I **slipped off**, gave our shoes back and had a Coke. An hour later we went back over to the two of them. They were standing there and hadn't agreed on the rules yet.

"Well, that was great," said Sven. "We should do this more often."

The two of them **broke off** their argument and looked at Sven.

"What do you mean?" asked Andreas.

"**Time's up**. You have to take your shoes back."

---

footwear – Schuhwerk; formal – förmlich;
lack of interest – Desinteresse;
to be precise – um genau zu sein;
ins and outs – *hier:* alle Details;
to contradict – widersprechen;
to develop – sich entwickeln;
to slip off – sich davonstehlen;
to break off – abbrechen;
Time's up. – Die Zeit ist um.

Sven went with Andreas, I went with Lucilla.

Both of them complained about each other, saying the other one was **to blame** for the fact that we hadn't played at all.

One thing they did agree on was that they found each other quite unbearable.

Now if that didn't sound like start of a beautiful friendship …

Monday 29th January

At first break Lucilla dragged me to the back of the school playground.

"It won't work out with Andreas," she told me as we stopped under the **chestnut tree**. "He talks too much. And too much rubbish at that."

"What about Max?" I asked. "He's nice!"

"Has he grown since I last saw him?"

"No, I don't think so. But **size** isn't important!"

"Oh come on, you don't believe that! Just think what we'd look like together. I mean, what would other people think? I mean, visually."

"You want a boyfriend to make you look good?"

"Yes. I want people to say: 'They make a beautiful couple!'"

---

to be to blame – schuld sein;
chestnut tree – Kastanienbaum;
size – Größe

Well, she's **got a point** there. Lucilla **astounded** me time and again.

"Haven't you got anyone else?" she asked.

"Man, Lucilla!" I said. "You need a bit of patience. Boys don't grow on trees."

Just then Philip fell out of the chestnut tree.

Lucilla looked at me in amazement.

I ran my eye over Philip. "Fifth grade," I concluded. "Too young for you, Lucilla. Forget it."

I took her by the arm and pulled her away from the chestnut tree.

Lucilla was still looking at Philip. "Was he **eavesdropping** on us?"

"No idea." I wasn't interested in the slightest. I was just thinking about whether we should put another advertisement in the newspaper, a proper one this time. "What do you think about putting a personal ad in a newspaper?"

Lucilla was horrified. "You haven't gone and done that, have you?" she asked.

"Well," I said, thinking about the episode with the pets section.

Did that **count**?

"Well?" asked Lucilla. "Yes or no?"

"No," I said, not wanting Lucilla to get into a state again.

---

to have a point – ein Argument haben;
to astound – erstaunen;
to eavesdrop – belauschen;
to count – zählen

"Thank God," she sighed in relief. "That would have been so embarrassing. It always looks so desperate."

"Well, it's not that **unusual**," I said, trying to **defend** my idea.

Lucilla shook her head **vigorously**. "You have to leave these things to **chance**," she explained. "It's all **fate**."

I gasped. "What are you talking about? Leave it to chance? You asked me – no, you **begged** me to find you a boyfriend!"

"I know I did! I mean, things like that don't just happen **by themselves**. You have to give them a helping hand. You have to play fate for me, **as it were**. And you have to arrange it for him and I to meet completely '**accidentally**'."

I frowned. "You know what, Lucilla. That's pretty complicated!" I protested.

Lucilla gave me a big smile. "But not for you, Jojo! If anyone can do it, then you can! You're great at things like that!"

I smiled, **flattered**. Maybe Lucilla was right? I'm sure she was.

---

unusual – ungewöhnlich;
to defend – verteidigen;
vigorous – energisch;
chance – Zufall; fate – Schicksal;
to beg – anflehen; by themselves – von selbst;
as it were – sozusagen;
accidental – zufällig;
flattered – geschmeichelt

In the afternoon Max called and asked if I wanted to go for a walk with him and the rabbit.

I was just about to tell him that Blacky had **given birth to** babies, but then I thought he might ask me for more money. After all, I'd only paid for one rabbit – though to tell the truth, I hadn't paid for anything at that point – and now we had five. So I kept my mouth shut in the end.

"So what about it? Do you want to come?" **persisted** Max.

"I would ..." I said **evasively**, "but I don't have time at the moment."

"So when do you have time?"

"Oh ... it could be a while."

"Okay, when?"

"Er, I don't know. Next month maybe?"

"Okay, when next month?"

"I mean, in the next months."

"More or less than six months?" asked Max.

Max seemed to have reached his limit. I was just about to say, "more like a year," when I heard his mum calling in the background: "Max! Ferdinand and Sebastian are here."

"Oh, you've got visitors!" I cried with a sense of relief. "Then I won't hold you up any longer."

"You're not holding me up. It's just two guys from my school," said Max, **playing** it **down**.

---

to give birth to – entbinden, *hier:* werfen;
to persist – beharren; evasive – ausweichend;
to play sth down – etwas herunterspielen

"Oh, right. Well, still, I hope you have a nice day and see you in ... Just a moment," I thought all of a sudden, "two boys from your school? Your age? Er ... just a second ..." This was my chance. I **jumped for joy** inside. Now all I had to do was keep my nerve. "Well, now you mention it, I happen to have a bit of free time right now," I said, putting on my charm.

"What do you mean?" asked Max, slightly confused.

"You wanted to meet up with me," I reminded him. "I've got time now."

"Now?"

"Yes, right now. Then I'm **fully booked** until a year from now," I added just to make his decision a bit easier.

Max hummed and hawed. "Well, I suppose I could ask my friends to come around another time ... Just a second ..."

"No! Wait! Max!" I screamed into the phone. I didn't mean it like that!

"Yes?" he asked shyly. He'd obviously heard my screams just in time.

"That would be **rude**, sending your friends home," I said, trying to sound **easy-going**. "Why don't you just bring them along?"

"Hm ..." Max thought about it.

---

to jump for joy – jubeln;
fully booked – ausgebucht; rude – unhöflich;
easy-going – unkompliziert

Oh please, please do what I say, I **prayed** to myself. Two new candidates for Lucilla. That would be perfect! One of them must be suitable! Why was Max hesitating so long?

"Is there a problem?" I asked, starting to get nervous.

"Well," said Max after a while, "it's just that they don't have any pets."

"No pets?" I squealed. "What's the problem with that?"

"I thought you were looking for people with pets," Max reminded me.

Time was running out. "Forget all the pet stuff," I **ordered** in my best no-nonsense voice. "Grab your friends and we'll meet up in half an hour at the shopping centre in front of the fountain. Okay?"

I had no patience left to be **tactful** and discreet. I wanted to see Ferdinand and Sebastian, so that Lucilla …

Lucilla! She had to come as well, of course. Panic.

"So, see you in a moment! Bye!" I called into the telephone, hung up, dialled Lucilla's number and told her to come to the shopping centre **at once**.

---

to pray – beten;
to order – befehlen;
tactful – taktvoll;
at once – sofort

Monday evening 29th January

"What's the big hurry?" asked Lucilla as she turned up in front of the fountain, slightly out of breath.

I gave her a big smile. "I've got a few candidates for you. You can **take your pick**!"

"Really?" Lucilla was **delighted**. "Where?"

I looked around. "They'll be here any second."

"You didn't tell them that I was ..."

"Of course not," I reassured her. "I arranged things **with the utmost skill**."

"Is that them?" Lucilla asked, pointing at a few boys who were hanging around in front of a sports' shop. "They look really sweet."

"No," I had to admit, "I don't think so."

"What do you mean, you don't think so? Don't you even know them?"

"Er, not really. But I know they're the right age for you," I added.

Lucilla **knitted her brow**. "I don't just take anybody! I'm not that desperate."

But I was. More than desperate in fact. I'd have taken any of them. For Lucilla.

"Hello, Jojo!" Max called from behind.

I spun around. "Hello, Max!" I cried effusively. "What a surprise!"

---

to take one's pick – sich etwas aussuchen;
delighted – hocherfreut;
with the utmost skill – mit größtem Geschick;
to knit one's brow – die Stirn in Falten ziehen

"Surprise?! But you said we should ..."

"I know, I know," I interrupted him and took a look at Max's friends.

One of them was **out of the question**: a mini-sized, **absent-minded** professor type with a **foible** for **brand names**. But his friend was really good looking.

"Hello," I said, turning to the good-looking one, "I'm Jojo and this is my friend, Lucilla."

Lucilla giggled. She always did that when she was nervous.

"Hi," was the only reaction from the guy.

"And what's your name?" I had to ask him. No manners. It was up to him to introduce himself.

"Ferdinand," said the mini-professor, taking my hand and shaking it vigorously, even though I hadn't asked him who he was.

"Aha," I nodded and turned back to the other one. He still said nothing. I turned back to Ferdinand. "And what's your friend called?" I asked.

"Max."

I gave Mr Cool my best smile and said, "Hello, Max!"

"I'm Max," said Max **wretchedly**. "That's Sebastian."

I looked at Ferdinand crossly. "Why did you say your friend's called Max?"

---

to be out of the question – nicht infrage kommen; absent-minded – zerstreut; foible – Schwäche; brand name – Markenname; wretched – kläglich

"Because Max is my friend. I hardly know Sebastian. He's not in my class."

"Oh. I see," I said, still feeling annoyed. But before I could **give voice to** my annoyance, Lucilla **tugged** at my sleeve. "Why did you ask the guy with the rabbit to come again?" she whispered into my ear. "I don't like him. But the other one is really sweet. The one called Sebastian."

As if I didn't know that myself. I hate it when Lucilla whispers things to me when other people are around. I've told her that a thousand times.

I pushed her away and hissed at her, "Stop whispering!"

"Oh, come on, Jojo!" she continued to whisper. "I can't possibly say that out loud!"

"Just say nothing."

"But how can you know who I ..."

"So what's up?" said Sebastian all of sudden, turning to Max. "Were we meant to come here and listen to girls whispering?"

"Nonsense," I intervened quickly. "We wanted to ... I thought we could ..." Blast, what were we doing here? I mean, I knew what Lucilla and I were doing there, but I could hardly say that to the others. "We wanted to start a club and we thought ... hey, maybe you'd like to join us."

Max and Ferdinand nodded enthusiastically.

Sebastian pulled a face. "What kind of club?"

---

to give voice to sth – etwas zum Ausdruck bringen;
to tug – zupfen

Boy, he's **fussy**. Who cares what kind of club? Lucilla was also looking at me with a big **question mark** in her eyes.

For some reason I looked at Ferdinand and said without thinking, "A Maths club."

What did I just say? A Maths club?! Oh, man, I have to see a doctor.

Sebastian **tilted** his head to one side. "You're joking?"

I nodded. "Yes, you're right," I said, trying to turn back time.

But Ferdinand had already **taken the bait**. "A Maths club," he cried full of enthusiasm, "that's great!"

Max also nodded **eagerly**.

"I don't have time for children's games. I'd rather go to training," said Sebastian and made a move to leave.

Lucilla stared at me in panic. I understood the look in her eyes perfectly well: don't let the guy go!

I grabbed Sebastian's sleeve. He scanned me from head to toe and then looked at my hand. I let go, but wasn't going to give up. "Lucilla has to go to training, too. Can you take her with you?"

Lucilla looked at me indignantly and hissed, "Jojo!"

---

fussy – pingelig;
question mark – Fragezeichen; to tilt – kippen;
to take the bait – in die Falle gehen;
eager – eifrig

Sebastian **scrutinised** me, then Lucilla. "Haven't you two got anything better to do?" he said and left without another word.

Max looked at me **sympathetically**. "He's not always like that," he apologized. "He messed up a Maths test recently and his dad said he'd cancel his basketball training if he doesn't **improve**."

"So, what now?" asked Ferdinand **keenly**. "Are we going to start a Maths club or not?"

I sighed. Empty-handed again. The only possible candidate had run off. It was more difficult than I thought. That is, unless Ferdinand was an option.

I turned to Lucilla. "What about you?" I asked emphatically. "Do you fancy a *Maths club*?"

Thank God she understood for once and answered with a **clear-cut** "No". Then, by way of an explanation, she added, "He's not my type."

I **winced**. The "no" had been quite enough information. She could have saved us the comment about not being her type. Boys aren't stupid.

"Shall we go for an ice cream?" Max asked me. "This time it's on me."

I smiled **appreciatively**. Max was okay really.

I looked at Ferdinand and Lucilla **enquiringly**.

---

to scrutinise – mustern;
sympathetic – mitleidig;
to improve – verbessern;
keen – eifrig; clear-cut – ganz klar;
to wince – zusammenzucken;
appreciative – dankbar;
enquiring – fragend

Lucilla raised her shoulders, undecided. Ferdinand said, "Sure. Then we can work through a few Maths problems."

With pleasure. I mean, I don't have anything better to do.

On the way to the ice-cream shop Lucilla spotted Carla hanging around with a group of boys.

"Would you be cross if I went over to Carla?" she asked tentatively. Then she whispered the reason why into my ear: "She knows a lot of sweet boys."

I was angry. "Oh, great, and what about me? Don't I know any sweet boys?" I had a go at her as quietly as possible.

Lucilla looked at Max and Ferdinand and then back at me and pulled a face of regret. "You understand, don't you?" she whispered and disappeared in the **direction** of the "sweet boys".

I took a deep breath and turned back to Max and Ferdinand. "Where were we?"

"Here. Where we stopped."

"No, I mean …"

"On the way to the ice-cream shop," Max reminded me. "We wanted to go for an ice cream."

"To start the Maths club," prompted Ferdinand.

My whole plan was down the drain. I nodded at a loss, and we trudged along to the ice-cream shop.

I was trying to decide if the **high point** of "what a

---

direction – Richtung;
high point – Höhepunkt

mess" had by now been reached or whether things could get any worse.

Then I suddenly found Sven standing in front of me. I immediately had a guilty conscience. Completely **uncalled for**, of course. I felt like I'd been caught red-handed.

"Hey, Jojo, what are you doing here?"

I pointed at the two boys. "Lucilla and I are going for an ice cream."

Sven looked at the boys and laughed. "And which of you is Lucilla?" he said, but he didn't wait for an answer. Instead he leant over to me and whispered, "I've got some bad news for you: you've got two boys **in tow**. No sign of Lucilla anywhere around."

"I know," I said, waving my hand dismissively and whispering an explanation to Sven: "I organized the boys for Lucilla."

"Oh right. Don't you think Lucilla should be here then?"

"I couldn't agree with you more," I said to Sven. "It's far from an ideal situation."

Sven looked at me lovingly.

I started to feel unsure of myself. "You do believe me, don't you?"

Sven grinned. "Every word. No one could **come up with** the things you do."

I sighed and nodded. How right Sven was.

---

uncalled for – unnötig;
in tow – im Schlepptau;
to come up with sth – sich etwas ausdenken

"We were just about to go for an ice cream," said Max shyly to Sven.

And Ferdinand added, "Yes, and we're going to start a Maths club."

"It would be great if you joined us," I suggested to Sven.

"I haven't got time," said Sven, pulling me to one side. "Listen, does you hanging around with other boys all the time belong to your brilliant plan to find Lucilla a boyfriend?"

"Yes."

Sven nodded. "Good. I just wanted to ask."

I looked at Sven **uncertainly**. How exactly did he mean that?

But before I could ask, he said, "I have to go. Bye!" and off he went.

I looked at Max and Ferdinand. They both looked at me **full of expectation**.

I sighed and set off. "Hello, ice-cream shop, here we come."

I decided the only thing that could save my day was to avoid the **setting up** of the Maths club – or at least make sure I didn't become a member of it. That was the only thing that could possibly give me some **sense of achievement**.

But even that was too much to ask for. I am now

---

uncertain – unsicher;
full of expectation – erwartungsvoll;
setting up – Gründung;
sense of achievement – Erfolgserlebnis

honorary chairwoman of the Maths club. We meet up once a week.

Why do things like that always happen to me?!

Tuesday 30th January

"I know where he goes training!" whispered Lucilla to me during German.

"Who?"

"Sebastian!"

"Hey, great!"

Lucilla nodded proudly. "We can go this afternoon!"

"I don't have time. I'm going out with Sven ..."

"Sven can wait. This is more important!"

I thought about it for a second and **came to the conclusion** that Lucilla was absolutely right. If Lucilla had a boyfriend at long last, then I could **devote** all my time to Sven. He surely would understand.

"Okay then, when shall we meet?" I whispered.

"Would the ladies at the back perhaps like to **share** their conversation with us?" Mrs Kielmeyer's voice **thundered** into our conversation.

---

honorary chairwoman – Ehrenvorsitzende;
to come to the conclusion – zu dem Schluss kommen;
to devote – widmen; to share – teilen;
to thunder – donnern

"Not really," I answered honestly.

I got extra homework for that.

Great, huh?

In the afternoon Lucilla and I **slipped over** to the sports centre. As we **crouched** against the wall and **peered** around the corner, I suddenly realized how stupidly we were **behaving**.

I stood up. "Why are we hiding?" I asked Lucilla.

"Ssshhh!" she hissed, pulling me back down. "So that Sebastian doesn't see us."

I was puzzled. "But you want to go out with him, or at least talk to him!"

Lucilla thought for a second. "Yeah, so what?"

"So what? Well, how's he meant to see you if you're hiding?"

Now it was Lucilla who stood up and thought hard about this. In the end she nodded. "You're right, Jojo," she concluded. "He has to see me. Otherwise it won't work."

So we ended up strolling into the sports centre, our heads held high.

Apart from us there was hardly anybody in the **stands**, which immediately made Lucilla want to **take cover** again.

---

to slip over – hinschleichen;
to crouch – kauern; to peer – spähen;
to behave – sich verhalten;
stands – Tribüne;
to take cover – in Deckung gehen

"Come on," I said, pulling her out from behind a **pillar**.

"But we're the only **spectators** here," moaned Lucilla.

"So what? Good for us. Then he can't miss you."

Lucilla sighed and stood up.

We looked for a seat and sat down.

Every time Sebastian got the ball, Lucilla **dug** her fingernails into my arm. "Oh, he's soooo sweet," she sighed.

And every time I **howled** with pain and pushed her hand away.

"I'm in love already!" she cried.

It was all a bit too quick for me. I was just about to say so when it occurred to me that it actually couldn't go quickly enough **as far as I was concerned**. After all, then I could be with Sven. Alone.

After the match we went onto the basketball court so that Lucilla could speak to Sebastian.

He came up to us, Lucilla did her best smile to smile – and he walked right past us. He hadn't even recognized us.

Lucilla burst into tears. It took a lot of effort to drag her out of the hall and calm her down outside.

Then Sebastian came out.

---

pillar – Pfeiler;
spectator – Zuschauer/Zuschauerin;
to dig – *hier:* krallen;
to howl – jaulen;
as far as I'm concerned – was mich angeht

I was angry with him. "Hey, Mr Maths Professor," I shouted at him, "shouldn't you be doing your homework?"

Lucilla **glared at** me furiously. "Why are you being so cheeky to him?" she hissed. "Then he'll never like me."

Sebastian came running up to us.

Lucilla quickly **wiped away** her tears and grumbled, "I've got a **swollen** nose and I look terrible."

"No, you don't, you look great," I lied.

"Do I know you?" asked Sebastian.

"No," I said, "and that's not going to change now."

Sebastian shook his head and walked off.

Lucilla gave me a **shove**. "Jojo!" she said reproachfully. "You've ruined everything now."

Before I could say she was right, Sebastian stopped in his tracks and came back to us with a grin on his face. "I know who you are ..." he said to me. "You're that weird girl from the shopping centre, the one who wants to start the Maths club."

"That's right," I said **without batting an eyelid**. And then I remembered Lucilla. "And this is my friend, Lucilla."

Sebastian nodded. "What are you doing here?"

---

to glare at sb – jmdn. anstarren;
to wipe away – wegwischen;
swollen – verquollen;
shove – Schubs;
without batting an eyelid – ohne mit der Wimper zu zucken

"Taking a look to see if your basketball is any better than your Maths," I answered. I was on top form.

Sebastian grinned. "Then you should come to the match on Saturday. That's when I'm at my best."

"What time?" I asked without hesitating.

"At three."

"Right. Three o'clock," I nodded, "We'll be there."

Sebastian shook his head with a **chuckle** and strolled off.

Lucilla stared at me in amazement. "How do you pull it off, Jojo? You're amazing!"

I nodded, pleased with myself. Oh yes, I can be really cool if I don't **fancy** the guy. That makes all the difference. Because when I think a boy is really great, I talk such a load of rubbish, it's like **toads** are **spewing** out of my mouth instead of words.

Lucilla beamed with delighted. "He invited me to the game!" she squealed. "Did you hear that? He wants to see me again!"

I frowned while I thought about this for a second. Had he invited Lucilla – and Lucilla only – to the match because he wanted to see her again?

I don't think so. But it didn't matter. Lucilla was happy, and she was already thinking about what to

---

to chuckle – in sich hineinlachen;
to fancy sb – auf jmdn. stehen;
toad – Kröte;
to spew – heraussprudeln

wear to a basketball game when you're friends with one of the players.

I think we're on the right track here.

I told Sven about my achievement in the **field** of Lucilla's love life and comforted him by saying he only had to **get through** this weekend and then I would finally have found Lucilla a boyfriend and our life together could begin again. Without Lucilla and without romance.

"And without Jojo-chaos and the **resulting** disasters," he added.

I generously chose not to hear his cheeky comment.

Saturday 3rd February

Okay, things can hardly go worse.

The day started badly this morning. Mum came up to me and said, "You have to look after Flippi today."

"I can't. I'm going to a basketball game."

"Then take her with you."

I pulled a face. "Can't you take her with you?"

Mum sighed. "Oskar's invited me out. I'm going

---

field – *hier:* Bereich;
to get through – durchhalten;
resulting – sich daraus ergebend

to the 'Blaue Reiter' **exhibition**. Flippi would really like to come, too, but putting Flippi in the same room as **priceless** paintings is not a good idea ..."

"**Got you**!" I nodded.

Then my mum started to giggle. "And besides, Oskar probably wants to apologize."

I **raised my eyebrows**, pleased to hear the news, and behind my back I **crossed my fingers** for Oskar. With a bit of luck he would choose the right words.

"And then there's the other thing ..." My mum started to hum and haw. "Unfortunately ..."

"What thing?"

She looked at me with a **grave** expression on her face and said **flatly,** "She found her magic bear."

"Oh no!" I cried, holding my hand up to my mouth in shock.

My mum nodded **knowingly**. "Keep an eye on her and let's try to solve the problem in the next few days. She might accidentally leave it lying around somewhere ..."

I grinned. "Are you going to make sure the bear disappears?"

My mum looked horrified. "Me?! Not at all. I'd never do a thing like that!"

---

exhibition – Ausstellung;
priceless – von unschätzbarem Wert;
Got you! – Verstanden!;
to raise one's eyebrows – die Augenbrauen heben;
to cross one's fingers – die Daumen drücken;
grave – ernst; flat – *hier:* tonlos;
knowing – vielsagend

I didn't say anything. I just looked at Mum and waited.

After a while she said sheepishly, "I thought maybe you could ... But I know nothing about it."

I nodded. I **got the picture**.

So I took Flippi to the basketball game.

Lucilla, Flippi and I sat in the stands, a lot of people were there. Flippi was being surprisingly **well-behaved**, apart from the fact that she poured her lemonade over the guy who **blocked her view** by sitting in front of her.

But she apologized as sweet as sugar. "I'm just so **clumsy**," she insisted. "Things like that happen to me all the time. But it's okay because if I go and buy another lemonade and spill it over you again then it doesn't matter. You're wet already."

The man didn't think about this for long. He just went and sat somewhere else, probably because Flippi looked so **convincingly** innocent that he couldn't even have a go at her properly.

Flippi was smiling from ear to ear. "Good, huh?"

I shrugged my shoulders. "Somebody else will sit there now."

"I don't think so," said Flippi and she poured

---

to get the picture – verstehen;
well-behaved – artig;
to block sb's view – jmdm. die Sicht versperren;
clumsy – tollpatschig;
convincing – überzeugend

some of the **remaining** lemonade onto the seat. "Watch out. The seat is wet," somebody commented as they passed by, looking for a free seat.

Flippi **got away with** it as ever. She had the best view of all.

The game was really exciting.

Lucilla waved to Sebastian. There's probably a more elegant way of doing this than Lucilla's. She just **swung** her arm through the air like a **windmill**. But I didn't say anything. She was in love. Anything goes.

"Come on, let's go down to the court," **pestered** Lucilla.

"Wait until the game's over."

"But I want to see him from closer up. After all, he did invite me. And he **waved** to me."

Lucilla was exaggerating there. The only thing Sebastian had done was run his fingers through his hair. Even a blind person wouldn't call that a wave. But hey!

When Sebastian's team won the game, Lucilla jumped to her feet and **cheered**.

Flippi leant over to me and said, "You know who made the **victory** happen …"

---

remaining – restlich;
to get away with sth – mit etwas durchkommen;
to swing – schwingen;
windmill – Windmühle;
to pester – *hier:* drängen;
to wave – winken; to cheer – jubeln;
victory – Sieg

"The better team?"

Flippi looked at me with a **pitiful** expression and shook her head. Then she looked at her bear knowingly and **waggled** it to and fro.

"Oh, right, of course," I was quick to say.

The crowd cheered. Giggling teenagers **shrieked** and threw cuddly toys onto the court. I've only ever seen that at a rock concert, but hey, **you live and you learn**.

Lucilla looked at her empty hands, then at Flippi's bear. She grabbed it and threw it onto the pitch with the words, "I'll buy you a new one."

It was a good shot. The bear hit Sebastian right on the head. Then he fell to the floor. The bear, that is, not Sebastian.

Flippi screamed. Lucilla held up her hand. "I'm sure it didn't hurt Sebastian," she said, alarmed.

"That was my bear, you fish face!" cried Flippi.

But Lucilla wasn't listening. She couldn't take her eyes off Sebastian. The players started to leave the court and so Lucilla rushed down from the stands. Then a drama **unfolded** before our very eyes:

Some girl ran up to Sebastian, threw her arms around his neck and kissed him. He put his arm

---

pitiful – mitleidig;
to waggle sth – mit etwas wedeln;
to shriek – kreischen;
you live and you learn – man lernt nie aus;
to unfold – sich entfalten, *hier:* sich abspielen

around her and the happy couple started walking off the court together.

Lucilla froze in her tracks. She turned around and had a go at me. “I told you we should have sat at the bottom!” she cursed. “Now someone’s **beaten me to it**.”

“She didn’t beat you to it. They clearly know each other. That’s his girlfriend, it’s obvious. Forget about him.”

Lucilla looked at the couple in disbelief. “How could he do this to me! He invited me!”

She stormed angrily down the steps. Flippi was still shouting at Lucilla about her bear. She followed her down the steps as well.

I knew I now had to **prevent** the worst. I **stumbled** after them but had difficulty in **keeping up** because now everybody was making their way down the steps.

I saw Lucilla reach the bottom. She stopped in front of Sebastian. I held my breath. What was going to happen now? But there was nothing to worry about. Sebastian and the girl just walked past Lucilla without even looking at her. They disappeared into the **crowd**.

Lucilla watched them pass, her mouth wide

---

to beat sb to it – jmdm. zuvorkommen;
to prevent – verhindern;
to stumble – stolpern;
to keep up – mithalten;
crowd – Menge

open. Flippi had caught up with her by now. She ran up to Lucilla, swearing at her, and **punched** her in the side. But Lucilla didn't respond. I hurried down to **protect** her from Flippi and comfort her about Sebastian, because I could see that Lucilla was now crying.

Then a boy came up to Lucilla, looked at her **compassionately** and put a teddy bear into her hands. It was Flippi's magic bear.

Flippi tore the bear out of Lucilla's hands, gave her a kick and disappeared.

Lucilla and the bear-**saviour exchanged** a few words, then he also disappeared.

By the time I finally got to Lucilla, all I could do was hand her a packet of **tissues**. But she just sobbed one more time, wiped away her tears and didn't say another word.

I didn't say anything either. I didn't know what to say. I took Lucilla in my arms and led her out.

Flippi was sitting outside. When she saw Lucilla, she gave her an **evil** look and mumbled something about a "bear kidnapper" and the "police".

It was all really depressing.

---

to punch – schlagen;
to protect – schützen;
compassionate – voller Mitgefühl;
saviour – Retter/Retterin;
to exchange – wechseln;
tissue – Papiertaschentuch;
evil – böse

Tuesday 6th February

I'm really worried about Lucilla. She hasn't said a word. At least, not about last Saturday and the disaster at the basketball game.

What worries me most is the fact that she's in a really good mood all the time. Non-stop for the last three days. That's not normal. She laughs, giggles and **chatters** away happily.

I have to do something about it. She's obviously **in a state of shock**. A trauma like that has to be talked about. It needs to be **healed**.

So today at break I cautiously **steered** our conversation onto the basketball game. "It was an interesting match on Saturday."

"Yes."

"But not that interesting."

"Depends on how you see it."

"It's not something I want to do every Saturday."

"I'm going again next Saturday!"

"Whaaat?!"

Lucilla looked a me, her eyes **bright**.

"But … you can't just …" I stuttered.

Lucilla shrugged her shoulders. "Why not? It's a **public event**. Anyone can go."

---

to chatter – plappern;
in a state of shock – in einem Schockzustand;
to heal – heilen; to steer – steuern;
bright – hell, strahlend;
public event – öffentliche Veranstaltung

I was flabbergasted. Poor Lucilla. A clear case of **suppression**. I hummed and hawed a bit but then decided to **tackle the problem head-on**.

"But Sebastian's got a ..." That was about as direct as I got.

Lucilla just waved her hand casually and said, "One mustn't take these things too seriously."

Good. It seemed she knew what I was talking about. But what did she mean by not taking these things too seriously? Sebastian had a girlfriend! She couldn't deny that.

"So you're really going again on Saturday?"

Lucilla nodded. "And to training. On Wednesday and Friday."

My jaw dropped. "Sebastian's got a girlfriend!" I cried out loud.

Why didn't Lucilla want to admit it?

She shrugged her shoulders. "So what?"

So what?! What was the matter with her? I had to stop her from going on Saturday. I couldn't let her do this to herself.

"Sven and I are going for an ice cream today. Do you want to join us?"

Did I seriously ask that? I started to wonder about my own sanity. But **what the hell**! Tough times need tough **measures**. This was about saving Lucilla.

---

suppression – Verdrängung;
to tackle a problem head-on – ein Problem direkt anpacken;
What the hell! – Was soll's!; measure – Maßnahme

Lucilla didn't seem able to decide. "I don't know. I haven't really got time."

"Lucilla, please!" I begged.

"Is it that important to you?"

"Yes!"

Lucilla sighed. "I'll see what I can do."

She'll see what she can do! I can't believe it. Lucilla's got it worse than I thought.

In the afternoon Sven picked me up and I told him straightaway about the worrying developments.

"She's in love with a boy who's got a girlfriend!" I said, bringing him up to date on the full **scale** of the drama.

Sven pretended to be horrified. "Oh my God, I knew it. I've always **suspected** it: She's in love with me!"

"Oh, Sven," I said, annoyed, "just drop it, will you! The boy's name is Sebastian and we have to do something about it!"

"Why?" said Sven, **unimpressed**. "Let her sort it out!"

"I can't do that. She's my best friend!"

Sven sighed. "Okay. What do you want to do?"

"Talk her out of Sebastian, of course."

Sven stopped and looked at me. "Let me just repeat this to check I've understood. You've **gone to**

---

scale – Maß; to suspect – ahnen;
unimpressed – unbeeindruckt;
to go to trouble – sich Mühe geben

a lot of **trouble** to find a boyfriend for Lucilla and you have in fact found one?"

"Yes."

"And now you want to talk her out of it?"

"Yes."

"Why?"

"Because he's not the right guy for her."

"Who says? Lucilla?"

"No, I do."

"Aha."

Then we both fell silent for a while. In the end Sven said, "Don't you think it would be better if you just didn't **get involved**?"

"No way. One of us has to **keep a grip on** things and make sure she doesn't **go off course**."

"And that person is you?"

"Hey, what are you trying to say?!"

"Why don't you find yourself a hobby?" suggested Sven **jadedly**. "A batik course? **Pottery**? Something where you can't cause too much trouble."

"Well, really! **That's** really **taking the biscuit**!"

Sven sighed. Why do people around me always have to sigh?!

"Come on, we have to hurry," I said, trying to **cheer** Sven **up**. "Lucilla's probably already waiting."

---

to get involved – sich einmischen;
to keep a grip on sth – etwas im Griff haben;
to go off course – aus der Bahn geraten;
jaded – erschöpft; pottery – Töpfern;
That takes the biscuit! – Das ist die Höhe!;
to cheer sb up – jmdn. aufmuntern

"Lucilla's waiting? Who for?"

"For us!"

"You can't be serious!" cried Sven and he sounded **genuinely** angry.

"If you don't want to join us, then just say!"

"I don't want to join you!"

"How can you say a thing like that?!"

Sven looked at me and I looked back at him stubbornly.

"I haven't got time now to argue with you," I said.

"What a shame. When would be a more **convenient** time for you? Why don't we make an **appointment**?"

Somehow Sven **threw me off course**. "OK," I said, "tomorrow afternoon would be just perfect."

Sven shook his head, turned around and just walked off. Home!

I was completely flabbergasted. What was going on? Did I do something wrong?

I was feeling really rather confused. I ran our conversation through my head and then I remembered that I'd just made a date with Sven so that we could have an argument. What a ridiculous idea!

But I didn't have time to deal with that now. First of all I had to protect Lucilla from herself.

So I ran to the ice-cream shop.

---

genuine – echt;
convenient – passend;
appointment – Termin;
to throw sb off course – *hier:* aus dem Konzept bringen

Lucilla wasn't there. I went in, sat down and waited. I ordered a tub of ice cream, ate it all up and continued to wait. But Lucilla didn't come.

Instead Max turned up. He spotted me as he was walking past the ice-cream shop and immediately came in.

"Hello, Jojo. Great to see you," he said cheerfully and sat down next to me.

"Hi, Max," I said, happy not to be sitting on my own any more.

"Yesterday was the Maths club meeting. Where were you?" asked Max.

Oh, blast! I'd forgotten that, of course. "I didn't have time. I had lots of homework. For school."

"Which subject?"

"Maths."

I could tell from the expression on Max's face that this wasn't the most convincing excuse not to come to the Maths club, but he was nice enough not to say anything, and I decided to go to the club meeting next week.

Max ordered himself a tub of ice cream. And one for me as well. Just the sight of more ice cream made me feel a bit sick, but I didn't want to disappoint Max, so I ate up my second **helping** as well.

"What are you doing here?" he asked all of a sudden.

I was slightly taken aback. I'd been so **wrapped**

---

helping – Portion; to be wrapped up in one's thoughts – gedankenverloren sein

up in my own thoughts that I hadn't said a word to poor Max the whole time.

"I'm waiting for Lucilla. My friend. You know her."

Max nodded.

I had an idea. "What do you think of Lucilla?"

Max shrugged his shoulders. "She's nice enough."

"Really?" I asked, pleased to hear this, and immediately started to think about how I could **fix** the fact that Max was too small.

As far as I could remember, that was the only problem Lucilla had with him. And the rabbit. But he didn't have that any more anyway. And now that things hadn't worked out with Sebastian, she might even give Max a chance.

"How's Blacky?" Max continued our conversation.

"Blacky?"

"The rabbit."

"Oh, he's fine."

"Good."

"So, you really think Lucilla's nice?"

"Yes."

"How nice?"

"Normal nice. I think most girls are nice."

"Have you got a girlfriend?"

Max turned red.

"Yes or no?"

---

to fix sth – *hier:* eine Sache hinbiegen, in Ordnung bringen

"No."

"Would you like one?"

Max shook his head.

I don't know whether I should **take** that **into consideration**. Sometimes you just have to **force** people to find their happiness.

"I **wonder** where Lucilla has got to," I said. Then something occurred to me: "Is Sebastian training again today?"

"I don't know. Maybe."

"Why don't we go for a walk?" I suggested and got to my feet, because I'd decided to go to the sports' centre to look for Lucilla.

Max looked unhappily at his tub of ice cream. It was only half empty.

"Right now?" he asked.

"Yes."

Max sighed, left his tub of ice cream behind and came with me. Our 'walk' led inconspicuously to the sports centre.

By then I was quite sure that Lucilla would be there, so I was surprised to find that she wasn't. In fact, no one was there.

"Are you looking for someone?" asked Max.

"No, I just wanted to go for a walk."

"To the sports centre?" Max frowned, but didn't say anything else about the matter.

---

to take sth into consideration – auf etwas Rücksicht nehmen; to force – zwingen;
to wonder – sich fragen

What if in the meantime Lucilla had gone to the ice cream shop and hadn't found me there?

"Let's go back to the ice-cream shop," I said rather nervously to Max, **turning on my heel**.

He looked at me despondently. To console him I said, "Maybe they haven't cleared away your ice cream yet and you can finish it off."

Max was too nice to reply. He just accompanied me back without a word of **complaint**.

Lucilla was standing in front of the door, waiting for us. She was in a really good mood. Over the moon in fact.

I **bit her head off** straightaway. "Where have you been? We were waiting for you!"

"We?" said Lucilla, looking at Max.

I didn't let myself be sidetracked. "Well?"

"I said I would see if I could make it." Then she grinned. "I got held up!" she added **coquettishly**.

Sebastian! She'd met up with Sebastian. Now it was official. Of course she didn't want to admit it to me, because I knew that he had a girlfriend. I was really shocked. How could Lucilla do something like that?! I had to open her eyes. But how?

Max was just the right person to help do the job. I turned to him and asked out of the blue, "How's Sebastian's girlfriend by the way?"

"Good." Max shrugged his shoulders.

---

to turn on one's heel – auf dem Absatz kehrtmachen;
complaint – Beschwerde;
to bite sb's head off – jmdn. anfahren; coquettish – kokett

I looked at Lucilla out of the corner of my eye. No reaction.

"How long have the two of them been together?"

"Six months I think," said Max.

"Aha. Could you imagine him leaving her for another girl?"

Max and Lucilla both looked at me in astonishment.

"You don't fancy him, do you?" asked Max.

"Me?!" I cried indignantly. "**Not on your life**. Besides, he's got a girlfriend. I'd never fall in love with a boy who's got a girlfriend," I said, keeping an eye on Lucilla.

Still no reaction.

"That's just not on," I added.

"Oh … I just thought … because you said … you asked about him," Max tried to apologize, stammering.

I waved my hand dismissively. "Forget about Sebastian," I said and added emphatically, "we should all forget about Sebastian."

"Do you want to have an ice cream or not?" asked Lucilla.

I'd lost my appetite. Besides, I hadn't done anything else for the past hour and a half except eating ice cream. After running to the sports' centre and back, I was now feeling sick. And the conversation with Max about Sebastian hadn't made me feel any better either.

---

not on your life – nie im Leben

"I want to go home," I whined.

"Okay," said Max.

"Why?" asked Lucilla.

My life is so terrible. Sven is angry with me. Lucilla is running after boys who are **spoken for** and Max ... yeah, what's with Max? Nothing. He's just nice. A small ray of hope in the darkness of my chaos.

Just a moment.

Perhaps something really could come of him and Lucilla! Don't give up too soon.

"Why not?" I changed my mind cheerfully. "Let's go and have an ice cream!"

Lucilla nodded. "That's what I'm here for."

"Okay," said Max. "Are we going to stay long? I mean, I don't know if it's worth ordering a tub of ice cream."

"It's worth it," I said, patting him on the shoulder.

It wasn't worth it in the end. Lucilla just won't let herself be **talked into** Max. Even though he's really nice.

She kept **referring to** some marvellous, sweet guy who she'd met and fallen in love with.

I thought it was a really stupid way of **turning down** Max.

---

spoken for – vergeben;
to talk sb into sth – jmdm. etwas aufschwatzen;
to refer to sb/sth – jmdn./etwas erwähnen;
to turn down – *hier:* abweisen

Besides, that Sebastian **has a real cheek** to meet up with Lucilla when he's already got a girlfriend.

No normal boy would do a thing like that, would they?

Wednesday 7th February

I racked my brains trying to think what kind of boy would have two girlfriends at the same time and why, but I couldn't come up with a single reason. So I decided I would just ask a boy.

Sven.

I gave him a call. It was only as he picked up the phone that I remembered we'd had an argument.

"Sorry, wrong number!" I said quickly and hung up.

I dialled again. "It wasn't the wrong number. It's just I've got a question. That is … if you're still talking to me," I said, trying to strike a **conciliatory** tone.

"What is it?"

"Can you imagine a boy going out with two girls at the same time?"

Sven had a **fit of laughter**.

---

to have the cheek to do sth – die Nerven haben, etwas zu tun;
conciliatory – versöhnlich;
fit of laughter – Lachkrampf

"Hey, what's so funny?" I grumbled. "That wasn't a joke. I need to know."

Sven calmed himself down in the end. "You're asking me?" he said.

"Yes. Well?"

"Jojo, that's exactly my problem: I always have to go out with two girls at the same time. And let me tell you: it's no fun. No one would do it **of their own free will**!"

"Oh, you just don't get it. I'm talking about Sebastian. He's got a girlfriend. And now he's going out with Lucilla as well."

"Just like me," insisted Sven.

"I'm being serious."

"So am I."

"We're not going to make any progress like this," I said, annoyed.

"Write the question down on your list," said Sven. "We can discuss it when we meet up for our argument."

I couldn't help laughing. Sven is really sweet. And I told him just that. "You're really sweet, Sven."

"I know."

"Forget about the argument, okay?"

"What argument?"

"Thanks," I laughed.

---

of one's own free will – freiwillig

A short time later I went into the kitchen and was just about to drop down into a chair, exhausted, when Flippi screamed at me. “No, Jojo!”

I jumped up, **panic-stricken**.

Flippi rushed over to the chair, wailing, “Did you hurt yourself?” and “Is everything okay, Paul?”

“Paul? Do our chairs have names now?” I said, looking at Mum for **support**.

She just sighed and rolled her eyes.

“What’s going on?” I demanded to know.

“You almost sat down on Paul!”

“So what?” I said. “Then I’ll just go and sit down on Peter …”

I went and sat down on another chair.

“Paul isn’t a chair!”

I looked at the chair and said, “Oh? What is he then?”

“Pff,” was all Flippi could say to me. Then she turned to the chair and said, “Come on, Paul, we’re leaving!” And with that she left the kitchen.

“Hey, Paul’s still here,” I said, pointing at the chair with a grin on my face.

“That’s not Paul. That’s a chair,” explained my mum. “Paul was sitting on the chair.”

“Have you two eaten something today which I missed out on? Or why else am I the only one not hallucinating here?”

Mum sighed. “Flippi has **conjured** herself a pet.”

---

panic-stricken – panisch;
support – Unterstützung; to conjure – herbeizaubern

Then she lowered her voice. "With the help of the magic bear. She found it again."

I felt a **pang of guilt**. I'd promised Mum to get rid of the bear, but with all my chaos, I'd completely forgotten.

"She was angry that I gave all the animals to Oskar. And that's why she's now got herself a kangaroo," sighed Mum.

"Paul?" I guessed correctly.

Mum nodded.

"How big is he?"

"About the same size as Flippi."

"Is he going to grow?"

"No idea."

"Paul," I said again and nodded to myself. Sure, why not. Paul the kangaroo.

"Am I the only one who can't see him?" I asked Mum.

My mum was rather embarrassed. "To be honest," she said wretchedly, "I did have the feeling I saw him two or three times. But I must have just been imagining things."

"For crying out loud!" I said and made my mum a strong cup of coffee.

---

pang of guilt – Anwandlung von Schuldgefühlen

"I didn't actually want to tell you about it until everything was a hundred **percent**, but it's just too wonderful," sighed Lucilla at school this morning. "I went to training again yesterday. He's sooo sweet."

"Lucilla!" I said, disappointed.

Lucilla looked annoyed. "I really don't know what your problem is, Jojo. Why can't you just be happy for me?"

I sighed. There was no way around it. "He's got a girlfriend!"

Lucilla beamed. "No, he doesn't. I asked him **specially**. I'm the only girl in his life! You see!"

"Are you sure?"

"Hey, the thing with Niko is never going to happen to me again. From now on I'll always ask **first thing**."

Yeah, yeah. But even that's no use if the guy doesn't tell the truth, I thought. It looked like I'd just have to force Sebastian to confess he already had a girlfriend.

"Can you take me along the next time you meet?" I asked **cunningly**.

Lucilla looked at me in surprise. "What a strange

---

percent – Prozent;
specially – extra;
first thing – sofort;
cunning – listig

suggestion, Jojo. Why would you want to be there when I meet up with my boyfriend?"

"Okay, forget it." I swallowed and tried not to be angry. But on the other hand I didn't want to give up too easily. "Not just me, of course. I mean, Sven and me. We could go out together, the four of us."

Lucilla thought about this for a second. "Hm. I'll have to ask him first."

"What?" I cried reproachfully. "You have to ask?"

"Of course, what do you think. I mean, it's his free time as well, you know, and it's not up to me alone who we go out with. He might want to be alone with me. I could understand that!"

I swallowed and wished I had something to bite on. "Then please ask him and let me know. We could go to the cinema together on Saturday," I suggested.

"I'll let you know," Lucilla promised. Then she looked at me **sternly** and said, "But not the cinema. That's no place for romance. Let's go bowling!"

I couldn't care less what we do. I had **a bone to pick with** Sebastian and it didn't make any difference where I did it.

At home, Flippi got into a state at lunch because I sat down in Paul's chair. What's more, she accused me of stepping on his foot.

---

stern – streng;
to have a bone to pick with sb – ein Hühnchen mit jmdm. zu rupfen haben

I had to **grovel** my apologies to **thin air** until Flippi **mercifully** told me that Paul had forgiven me.

I was really annoyed and decided to get rid of the magic bear **once and for all** – just in case Paul got any little brothers or sisters. There was also the chance that Paul might disappear when the bear had gone.

I whispered to my mum that she should keep Flippi in the room until I came back and then I disappeared. I **turned** Flippi's entire room **on its head**, but found nothing.

The good thing about searching for something in Flippi's room is that you never have to **tidy up** afterwards. Her room is complete chaos anyway, and Flippi doesn't even notice if everything is lying around all over the place. During the **hunt** I discovered two of my pullovers, five CDs and a Maths book of mine. Everything **except** the magic bear.

I went back into the kitchen to rescue Mum. She was sitting on a chair, reading a story to Flippi and Paul.

"Read that part again," Flippi said, just as I came in, "that's Paul's favourite part."

---

to grovel – katzbuckeln;
thin air – das Nichts; merciful – gnädig;
once and for all – endgültig;
to turn sth on its head – etwas auf den Kopf stellen;
to tidy up – aufräumen;
hunt – *hier:* Suche;
except – außer

Mum obediently **reread** a **section**, then sighed, leant over the empty chair with a smile and said, "Paul, if you want, I can read to you this evening, but right now I have to clean the kitchen."

Flippi didn't react.

Mum smiled again at the empty chair. "That is, unless you want to help me?"

Flippi looked at my mum pityingly. "Paul left the kitchen ages ago," she told her and also disappeared.

Mum dropped onto Paul's chair, looking very unhappy. Now I had to tell the poor woman even more bad news.

"Listen," I whispered to my Mum, "I can't find it anywhere. It's **disappeared off the face of the earth**!"

"What has?"

"Flippi's magic bear!"

Mum turned red and looked down. "Er … you don't need to look any more, Jojo," she said, embarrassed.

"You haven't …?" I said, but Mum stopped me with a look.

Oh man, I couldn't believe it. My own mother!

And it hadn't even helped. Paul was still living with us. We weren't going to get rid of him that easily.

---

to reread – noch einmal lesen; section – Teil;
to disappear off the face of the earth – wie vom Erdboden verschwinden

In the afternoon I had to go shopping for my mum. Going shopping for my mum is a pure intelligence test. She always gives me a shopping list, but this doesn't help me in knowing what I'm meant to buy. They're not lists, more like short stories.

For example: *Milk, the one with the blue cow on the* ***packaging****. And if there's no more milk with the blue cow, then bring orange juice. Actually, buy some milk,* ***no matter what****. If not with the blue cow, then another one. And orange juice, too. Anyone, but* ***preferably*** *the one in the carton with the clever little top. And don't forget the strawberry* ***jam****. The one that looks like it's* ***home-made****, please, with the white* ***bonnet****. I mean, the bonnet is on the lid, not on the jam. If you see a jam jar with any white on the* ***surface****, then don't take it. It's* ***mould****. If you don't like strawberry jam, then take something else.*

When I read her shopping list, I always have the feeling that Mum is standing right next to me giving me instructions.

Flippi came shopping with me. And Paul, too.

My mum insisted that I take Paul as well. "I don't want to have him here in the home when Flippi's not around," she explained quietly to me. "I can't even see him. It's a bit **creepy**."

---

packaging – Verpackung; no matter what – egal welche;
preferably – am besten; jam – Marmelade;
home-made – selbst gemacht;
bonnet – Haube; surface – Oberfläche;
mould – Schimmel;
creepy – unheimlich

I looked at my mum in amazement but **spared** her my thoughts.

As I went out of the front door, I heard my mum sigh, "Why did God have to punish me with children? Wouldn't another **flood** have been enough?"

Friday 9th February

Yesterday turned out well in the end, **despite** everything. Flippi put Paul in the **shopping trolley** in the supermarket, but Paul took up so much space that Flippi only let me use a tiny corner for our shopping items.

Shortly afterwards I was standing in front of the shelves, looking for the right brand of milk. I'd just spotted a blue cow when I heard a **cutting** voice behind me: "Don't forget the **porridge**. It's an **essential** part of any small child's or idiot's **diet**."

Carla. That **malicious** cow!

"Thanks for the tip," I said. "Why don't you come over for breakfast some time then?" Then I was

---

to spare sb sth – jmdm. etwas ersparen;
flood – *hier:* Sintflut;
despite – trotz;
shopping trolley – Einkaufswagen;
cutting – schneidend; porridge – Haferflocken;
essential – wesentlich;
diet – Ernährung;
malicious – gehässig

annoyed with myself because I'd said I wouldn't **take** any **notice of** Carla.

I moved on in search of cornflakes, my main source of nutrition. They were standing at the end of the **aisle**, arranged in a tall pyramid.

I'd seen this moment a thousand times in stupid films. And each time I saw it, I always thought: things like that don't happen in real life.

But they do.

I didn't take the packet from the very bottom – I'm not that stupid – but as I reached up to take the packet from the top, I **lost my balance** and stumbled into the cornflakes pyramid.

The first person on the scene was, of course, Carla. She laughed her head off. "That'll make a great story in school tomorrow: 'Bed-wetter **buried** in cornflakes'."

I got to my feet, furious, and as the **branch manager** hurried over, I shoved a packet of cornflakes into Carla's hand and said, "I don't think that's funny, pulling out the bottom packet. Why don't you grow up?"

That left Carla completely speechless.

I turned to the branch manager. "She's outrageous!" I said, looking at Carla. "She always does

---

to take notice of sb/sth – jmdn./etwas beachten;
aisle – Gang;
to lose one's balance – sein Gleichgewicht verlieren;
to bury – begraben;
branch manager – Filialleiter

that. And then she says it had nothing to do with her."

"It had nothing to do with me!" said Carla **in indignation**.

"You see," I nodded to the branch manager and walked off.

I heard the **heated** argument, but Carla didn't stand a chance. She had to put the pyramid back up on her own.

I knew perfectly well that what I'd done was really mean, but Carla deserved it. I couldn't just wait until her hair grew back. Otherwise I'd **lose my touch**.

Flippi gave me a nudge and winked at me with a grin on her face. "I'm proud to be your sister."

Unfortunately, because of events, I'd left the trolley next to the ex-cornflakes pyramid and we had to go to another shop. I wasn't going back, that's for sure. So I had to start with the shopping list all over again.

All of a sudden, something occurred to me. "Is Paul with us?" I asked Flippi, panic-stricken.

"Of course!" said Flippi with a nod of her head. Then she giggled. "Didn't you see the way he kicked Carla in the **shins** just now."

What a good little kangaroo Paul is!

---

in indignation – empört; heated – hitzig;
to lose one's touch – aus der Übung kommen;
shin – Schienbein

Saturday 10th February

Okay, today is the moment of truth for Lucilla.

I was feeling really awful. I felt so sorry for Lucilla. But there was no other way. It was all so **futile**. I had to bring the game to an end.

Four o'clock in front of the bowling centre. My wonderful, **darling** Sven was even willing to get through this day together with me.

"It's really nice of you to come with me."

"Hey, what else would you expect? After all, I've got a **box** for the third act of this drama. I wouldn't miss it for the world."

"Am I right in thinking you're not taking this particularly serious?"

"But that's okay," Sven reassured me. "After all, you're taking it seriously enough for the two of us!"

On the way to the bowling centre we **bumped into** Max.

As Max saw me and Sven with our arms around each other, he seemed to be a bit embarrassed. I was as well all of a sudden.

Only Sven wasn't. "Hello, Max!" he said cheerfully.

Max relaxed a bit. "Hello," he replied politely and looked at me.

---

futile – sinnlos; darling – *hier:* wunderbar
box – *hier:* Logenplatz;
to bump into – zufällig treffen

I hadn't said anything yet. Sven also looked at me and then pretended to be really shocked. "Urgh! What's that hanging on my arm?"

Sven jumped away from me, still pretending to be horrified. "I don't know!" he said, shaking his head at Max. "Girls these days! If you just look away for a second, they **stick** to your arm. Do you have the same problem?"

"No," said Max, sounding slightly despondent.

Sven saw straightaway that his joke had backfired, so he pointed at me and said, "Count yourself lucky. This one here's a right **handful**."

That was more than cheeky from Sven, but it broke the ice. Max gave a smile. Sven and Max exchanged a few words while I **kept mum**.

That is, until I heard Max say, "I have to go. Sebastian's coming around in a minute to do Maths with me. He messed up another test."

I was completely flabbergasted. "What? He's coming around now? To your place?"

"Yes," said Max tentatively, obviously surprised by my **unconcealed** interest for Sebastian in the presence of Sven.

"That can't be true!" I moaned.

Max was now even more embarrassed. "Well, he said that he'd try to come, but that something

---

to stick – kleben;
handful – *hier:* Nervensäge;
to keep mum – sich in Schweigen hüllen;
unconcealed – unverhohlen

might **come up**," stammered Max. "I'd better go home anyway. Just in case he comes."

Max then disappeared, **somewhat** faster than necessary. In fact, it looked more like he was running away.

"He's really nice," said Sven. "But I think you confuse him."

He wouldn't be the first, I said to myself, feeling **down**. Then I thought about what I was going to do to stop Sebastian.

A minute later we bumped into Sebastian. With his girlfriend. They had their arms around each other.

That **was** just **the limit** for me! I shouted "Stop!" at them and stepped into their path.

Sven tried to hold me back by the sleeve, but I was too quick. There was no time to explain the situation to Sven.

"What do you think you're doing?" I said to Sebastian **without beating about the bush**.

"Who are you?" asked Sebastian **indifferently**.

It took me a moment to answer the question because I was so gobsmacked that he didn't recognize me for a second time. Pretty depressing really. And it didn't help me be any nicer to him.

---

to come up – dazwischenkommen;
somewhat – ein wenig; down – deprimiert;
to be the limit – der Gipfel sein;
without beating about the bush – ohne Umschweife;
indifferent – gleichgültig

"Right," I said to Sebastian **patronizingly** – well, as patronizingly as you can be when you're looking up to someone two heads taller than you – "I'm now going to do your girlfriend a big favour ..." Then I turned to her and explained, "In about two minutes Sebastian will apologize to you and say that he has to go."

His girlfriend looked at me **unruffled**. "He already told me," she said coolly. "He's going around to his sick auntie's. He often does that."

"His aunt! That's a good one!" I said, laughing out loud. Sebastian **turned bright red**. "No, that's not it. Today he'll say he has to go and do Maths with Max."

Sebastian was flabbergasted. He looked at his girlfriend, **overcome with remorse**. "That's true," he said guiltily. "I'm sorry, Britta. The thing about my aunt isn't true."

"So why did you say it then?"

Sebastian shrugged his shoulders. "I just didn't want you to know that I'm taking help in Maths. It's not exactly cool."

Britta looked at him lovingly. "Oh really, Basti, I don't care about things like that." She **squeezed up to** him and he put his arm around her.

---

patronizing – herablassend;
unruffled – unbeeindruckt;
to turn bright red – knallrot werden;
overcome with remorse – zerknirscht;
to squeeze up to sb – sich an jmdn. schmiegen

I was a bit confused for a second, but I **didn't lose sight of my goal**. "Hold on!" I said, putting a stop to their **cuddling**. "He's not going to learn Maths. He's going to the bowling centre to spend a nice afternoon with his other girlfriend."

Britta's jaw dropped. She stared at Sebastian in disbelief.

"And that's been going on for a while," I added.

"Is that true?"

"Er ... no. I have no idea what this **half-wit** is talking about. I wouldn't lie to you."

"Oh?" I said quickly. "And what about your sick aunt?"

"Exactly," cried Sebastian's girlfriend, pushing away her boyfriend **in dismay**. And without saying another word she stormed off.

Sebastian looked at me and said, "You belong in a clinic!" Then he ran after Britta.

"So now I've finally put an end to the **nightmare**! Ha!" I turned to Sven who was at least as flabbergasted as Sebastian and his girlfriend. "Now he hasn't even got one girlfriend. **Serves him right**! **You can't have your cake and eat it**!"

---

to not lose sight of one's goal – sein Ziel nicht aus den Augen verlieren;
to cuddle – kuscheln; half-wit – Schwachkopf;
in dismay – bestürzt;
nightmare – Albtraum;
Serves him right! – Selbst schuld!;
You can't have your cake and eat it. – Man kann nicht auf zwei Hochzeiten tanzen.

"Jojo, that really wasn't a good idea."

"Oh? You boys are all the same!"

"And don't even think about starting a row with me," Sven warned me.

When we got to the bowling centre, Lucilla was already there, waiting expectantly on her own.

"You see," I said to Sven reproachfully, "there she is, **clueless** and lonely." Then I said "hello" to Lucilla and took her in my arms to **console** her.

"Hey, be careful! Don't ruin my hairdo," Lucilla **fended** me **off**.

Oh, poor clueless Lucilla. Her hairdo was the least of her problems. How could I break it to her gently?

"We have to wait for a bit. Jonas had to do something in town at lunch. He'll be here in a minute," sighed Lucilla.

I sighed. I'd already seen what "Jonas" had to do!

Jonas?! Man, Sebastian had even made up a name for himself. That only made me even more annoyed.

"Listen, Lucilla, I have to tell you something! But please, don't get worked up about it."

Sven tugged at my arm. "Jojo, I think you should …"

"No," I pushed him away, "I'm sorry. I can't keep silent any longer. Lucilla has to know the truth."

---

clueless – ahnungslos; to console – trösten;
to fend sb off – jmdn. wegstoßen

Lucilla looked at me with wide-open eyes. "What's the matter?"

I **cleared my throat** and took a deep breath. "Well …"

Sven interrupted me again. "Jojo, I think you're making a mistake."

"No. I've **thought** everything **through**."

"What on earth is it?" Lucilla was growing impatient.

"Well, to keep it short: dear, young Sebastian – or should I say Jonas? – is leading a …" I stopped talking and watched in amazement as Lucilla suddenly ran off and threw herself around some boy's neck. "… double life," I said quietly, ending my sentence. "Who on earth is that?" I asked Sven, horrified.

Sven grinned slightly. "Jonas maybe? Lucilla's new boyfriend?"

"But no," I stammered. "Sebastian is her … she said … didn't she?" Sven looked at me full of pity and opened his arms to console me.

"Oh my God!" I screamed as I suddenly realized what I'd done. "It's not Sebastian at all," I cried, **clinging to** Sven. "It's …"

"Jonas," Sven prompted me. "His name is Jonas."

---

to clear one's throat – sich räuspern;
to think sth through – sich etwas gut überlegen;
to cling to sb – sich an jmdn. klammern

Lucilla and Jonas came over to us. Lucilla wanted to introduce her new boyfriend to us, but I was pressing my face up against Sven's **chest** and didn't want to see anybody.

"What's wrong with her?" Lucilla asked Sven.

"She's not feeling very well. Too many good deeds for one day."

"Oh my God!" I moaned into the collar of Sven's jacket. "Take me home!"

"I'm sorry, I think we'd better go," said Sven to Lucilla and Jonas. "Maybe we can meet up another time, okay?"

Sven led me away.

"Are we alone?" I asked.

"Pretty much."

I took my face out of the collar of Sven's jacket and stared at Sven. "I've just **destroyed** a happy relationship. I thought ... but Lucilla said ..." I took a big swallow. "I just ..."

Sven nodded and stroked my hair. "... you just wanted to help?"

I nodded.

"How did that happen?" I asked miserably.

Sven just looked at me.

I came to a conclusion: "It was all Lucilla's fault!"

"Did she actually say she was going out with *Sebastian*?"

"Not in as many words. I just **presumed**. She was

---

chest – Brust; to destroy – zerstören;
to presume – annehmen

always talking about a basketball player … how could I know …?"

"That there's more than one basketball player in a basketball team?" Just as well Sven never lost his sense of humour.

"What am I going to do now?"

"The same thing you have to do every few weeks," grinned Sven. "You have to go to everybody **involved** and apologize for the chaos you've caused."

"Can't you do that for me? It's sooo embarrassing. I'm going to ask Mum if we can move house!"

"How about a **witness protection programme**?"

"Stop making jokes about it!" I wailed.

"Who was that boy anyway?" I asked myself.

"Do you mean Jonas?"

"Yes."

"No idea."

He **looked familiar** to me. I'd seen him before. But where?

"What am I going to do?" I whined to Sven. "I can't go to Sebastian and his girlfriend and apologize."

Sven looked at me strictly.

I **stamped my foot**. "Do you realize how bad what I've done is?" I said, annoyed. "I can't just …"

---

involved – beteiligt;
witness protection programme – Zeugenschutzprogramm;
to look familiar – bekannt vorkommen;
to stamp one's foot – mit dem Fuß aufstampfen

"What?"

"Oh, man, you're a big help."

"If you want, I can help you by coming with you and standing next to you. Like a **lie detector**. Just to make sure you don't tell any **tall stories** and cause more trouble."

"Where do I have to go?"

"To Max!"

"What's Max got to do with it?"

"I guess that's where the victim of your rough **justice** is sitting right now. That is, unless Sebastian is still running after his girlfriend in despair."

"Can't I just call?"

Sven put his arm around me and pulled me along. "Where does Max live?" he asked.

For a second I thought about giving the wrong address, but then I gave in and **succumbed** to my fate.

All of a sudden, I felt sorry for Sven. "And you, poor thing, are going out with me!"

Sven sighed. "Yes, I know. It's tough."

"Look, I can understand it if you don't want to have anything to do with me any more," I whined, **on the brink of** tears.

"What do you mean? My life would be really bor-

---

lie detector – Lügendetektor;
tall story – Märchen;
justice – Gerechtigkeit;
to succumb – sich beugen;
to be on the brink of sth – kurz vor etwas sein

ing then. Now that Lucilla has got a boyfriend and we can finally go out together alone."

I sniffled.

Sven gave me a big hug and kissed me.

Sebastian really was at Max's place. My eyes were still swollen from crying as I asked if I could have a word with him. Sven took Max to one side and told him what this was all about. It was obvious what they were talking about, because every now and again they burst into **muffled** laughter.

Sebastian listened to my story and kept shaking his head. "I suggest you tell all that to Britta as well," he said in the end. "And you can do me a big favour as well."

"Anything," I agreed without hesitating. "What do you want?"

"Just **steer clear of** me when you see me, don't talk to me, never make friends with Britta, and think about moving to another town." He shook his head. "And you only meant well! What would happen if you wanted to cause trouble?!"

I decided I had now **suffered** enough. "Now don't exaggerate," I protested. "I'll explain everything to your girlfriend, and that's the end of that. Everybody makes mistakes. And I always apologize."

Sven had obviously heard that the conversation

---

muffled – gedämpft;
to steer clear of sb – einen Bogen um jmdn. machen;
to suffer – leiden

had grown somewhat louder, and he rushed in to us to pull me away from Sebastian. "That's enough," he said. "**Call it a day**, Jojo."

Then Sven said goodbye to Max. They seemed to be good friends judging by the way they patted each other on the shoulder so cheerfully.

Max grinned at me and I had the feeling that he was looking at me through different eyes all of a sudden.

Pah, but who cares? I just want to go home.

I'll pour my heart out to Paul. He'll understand.

Sunday 11th February

No, the world isn't a better place the next day. That's just a stupid **saying**.

In fact, I found everything even more embarrassing than the day before. But at least I didn't have a guilty conscience after having apologized. Yesterday evening I called Britta. Sebastian had already told her everything, but it was probably a good thing that I **confirmed** things, too.

So if the two of them ever **split up**, it's got nothing to do with me.

---

to call it a day – *hier:* es gut sein lassen;
saying – Spruch;
to confirm – bestätigen;
to split up – sich trennen

I set about calling Lucilla this morning **with a heavy heart**. While the phone was still ringing, I remembered that I didn't have to apologize to Lucilla at all. In fact, I didn't even have to say a word about the whole mess.

When she picked up the phone, I **was my old self**.

"Hey, Lucilla, how are you?" I said as happily and **uninhibited** as possible.

"The question is, how are you?" she asked anxiously.

"Great," I lied.

"What was all that about yesterday?" Lucilla wanted to know. "Why did you ask Sven to take you home all of a sudden?"

"Oh, nothing much … I just had … something in my eye," I said.

Lucilla didn't respond.

"Something big," I added to give my explanation some **credibility**.

"Oh, right."

I now had to change the subject quickly. "So, now it's your turn. Tell me about Jonas. Where did you meet him? What's he like? Have you already kissed?"

"No."

"No what?" I had to ask again. You can never ask

---

with a heavy heart – schweren Herzens;
to be one's old self – ganz der/die Alte sein;
uninhibited – unbefangen;
credibility – Glaubwürdigkeit

Lucilla more than one question at a time. It always confuses her. I had to start from the beginning. "Where did you meet him?"

"Oh, come on, you know that. You were there at the time!"

"What? When?"

"At the basketball game," giggled Lucilla. "Flippi's bear played **Cupid**."

The magic bear! **Well I never**! So it is good for something then!

"He's really sweet! And so romantic!" Lucilla went into raptures.

I was still thinking about the magic bear, so I needed a few seconds to realize she was talking about Jonas.

"He's just the sweetest thing," sighed Lucilla. "A real Prince Charming. The greatest guy in the world!"

Aha? What's that supposed to mean? That I got **lumbered with** second best in Sven?

"Have you already kissed him?" I asked to dampen Lucilla's enthusiasm.

I was annoyed by her **fervour**. And to be honest, I was also feeling annoyed because I'd spent the past few weeks desperately trying to find a boyfriend for Lucilla and then she goes and finds

---

Cupid – Amor;
Well I never! – Sieh mal an!;
to lumber sb with sth – jmdm. etwas aufhalsen;
fervour – Inbrunst

one on her own. And **in the process** I'd **made a** complete **fool of myself**. Well, marvellous. And on top of that I now have to be happy for her.

Lucilla didn't let her enthusiasm be dampened. "You must be joking! We've only just met. You have to wait for the right moment to kiss. Everything has to be perfect. It has to be really ... "

" ... romantic," I finished her sentence for her.

"But you're not in a good mood at all, Jojo!" said Lucilla.

"My eye's still hurting."

"Your eye?"

"From yesterday. I got something in it."

"Hm."

"I'll give you a call later on," I suggested to Lucilla and she agreed.

"I might not be here," she giggled. "Jonas wants to go ice skating with me."

"How romantic!" I said after I'd hung up.

Yes, I was angry. You make an effort to do something good and what comes of it? Nothing but trouble.

That was definitely the last time I look for a boyfriend for somebody else!!!

---

in the process – dabei, im Verlauf;
to make a fool of oneself – sich blamieren

Monday 12th February

I made up with Lucilla today. Well, **strictly speaking**, she didn't actually know we'd **fallen out**. I wanted to hold out a bit longer, but it was so boring in school, I really needed a change.

Lucilla is on cloud nine at the moment. Jonas seems to be a really nice guy.

But when I asked her if she wanted to meet up in the afternoon, she said, "I'm meeting up with Jonas."

"I don't mind," I said, "I'll come along with you."

"I'd rather you didn't. At least, not yet. When Jonas and I know each other a bit better maybe. Strangers always **disturb** a relationship at the beginning."

Uuh! Strangers. Now I'm a stranger all of a sudden, am I? I decided to have another argument with Lucilla.

"Well, actually," I said curtly to Lucilla, "I haven't got time anyway. I have to go to the Maths club."

That was telling her.

---

strictly speaking – genau genommen;
to fall out – sich streiten;
to disturb – stōren

Tuesday 13th February

My arguments with Lucilla never last long.

When she asked me this morning, "What's new?" I decided to be friends with her again.

Hm, what is new? Not a lot really. Sven and I hang out together practically every day since Lucilla's not around and I'm back to my old self. We have a lot of fun. But I couldn't say that to Lucilla.

"Yesterday was Maths club. It was great."

"Aha," said Lucilla, unimpressed, waiting for more interesting news.

"Max says hello," I lied.

Lucilla was pleased. "He's a really nice guy," she said.

"Yeah, he is."

"It's a shame he doesn't have a girlfriend."

"You're right."

"He just needs someone short," thought Lucilla out loud.

I nodded.

"Tomorrow is Valentine's Day. The day for lovers," **crooned** Lucilla. "We're doing something really romantic."

"Oh really, what?" I asked the expert in romance.

"We're going to the cinema!" said Lucilla with a big smile.

"To the cinema?!" I cried. "Since when is that romantic?"

---

to croon – schnulzen

"Oh, Jojo," giggled Lucilla, "you really have no idea."

I looked at her with wide open eyes.

"It's dark in the cinema. You spend the whole time sitting close to one another. You can hold hands!" explained Lucilla.

I gasped but didn't say a word.

"And what are you two doing?" asked Lucilla.

"Something much more romantic!" I replied defiantly.

"What then?"

"Uhm ..." I had to think about this because Sven and I hadn't actually made any plans.

"Come on, tell me," insisted Lucilla.

"Er, we're ..." I stammered, desperately racking my brains.

What was my family doing tomorrow? Flippi was organizing the Snail Olympics with Paul. Doesn't sound too romantic. Mum and Oskar wanted to make a **hutch** for the rabbits. Also not exactly romantic. My life is just so unromantic! But who cares about Valentine's Day anyway? It's just a load of rubbish.

"We're **giving** Valentine's Day **a miss**," I told Lucilla after careful consideration.

"Really? And you call that romantic?"

"Yeah, of course, why not?"

"Oh, Jojo, we really must have a serious talk some time," sighed the expert on romance.

---

hutch – Stall; to give sth a miss – etwas auslassen

Wednesday 14th February

That's it. It's over. Finished. Done with. Life hates me.

It plays the dirtiest tricks on me!

I met up with Lucilla before school started this morning. She was waiting for me in front of the **gates**.

"There you are at last," she cried, giggling to herself.

"What's the matter?" I asked in surprise.

"I've got the idea of the **century**!"

"What is it?"

"It's such a great idea!"

"I believe you. Come on then, tell me!"

"Max is a really nice guy," said Lucilla.

"Yes, he is," I nodded.

"I think we should look after him a bit, take him along when we go out and stuff."

"I have no problem with that."

"Good. Because I've got an idea." Lucilla giggled. "To be honest, I was amazed that I came up with such a brilliant idea all on my own. That's never happened to me before. You'll be really impressed. Won't you?"

"Er, tell me what it's about and then I'll tell you if I'm impressed."

"Oh, you will be, I'm quite sure about that!" Lucilla reassured me.

---

gate – Tor; century – Jahrhundert

Unfortunately, she still hadn't told me what it was all about. And it looked like she wasn't going to do so either, because she was just looking at me expectantly.

"So, what is it then?" I prompted her.

"What is what?"

"Oh, Lucilla, the idea! The fantastic idea! Just spit it out, will you!"

"Oh, right. Sure. OK. Well, try and guess!"

"No!" I begged in despair.

"Oh, please! Please try and guess!"

I knew what I had to do. I crossed my fingers that I wouldn't get it right the first time around. "You're going to cut your hair short?"

Lucilla ran her fingers through her hair. "No. What makes you think that?" she said, surprised. "Or do you think short hair would **suit me** better?"

I howled out loud. "No. Please, just tell me what the idea is."

"Oh my goodness," giggled Lucilla. "I'd almost forgotten!"

I nodded and waited.

"You'll love it, Jojo!"

I tried to remain calm because I knew Lucilla wasn't doing it on purpose and the more I got worked up, the longer it would take for her to finally tell me what it was about.

So I just kept waiting. Smiling amiably.

And then the time came.

---

to suit sb – jmdm. stehen

Lucilla was **grinning like a Cheshire cat**. "You know today is Valentine's Day," she started, "and that's really romantic and stuff. And whenever I see couples kissing, I always think …"

"… and who's going to kiss me?" I interrupted her.

"No," said Lucilla, shaking her head. "I'm sure Jonas will kiss me at some point. No, I always think: And who's going to kiss Max? And I'm sure Max sometimes thinks: And who loves me?"

I nodded. Maybe, but I still didn't know what Lucilla was getting at.

She took a deep breath and **emphasized** each and every word: "And that's what made me think: Max needs a girlfriend."

I nodded again. Okay, as far as I was concerned, fine. "And why are you telling me this?"

"Well, Jojo, it's obvious: You have to find Max a girlfriend! If anyone can make it happen, then you. You've got the **knack**."

I stared at Lucilla and had to hold onto the school gate. Then everything went black.

"But don't forget," Lucilla reminded me, "she has to be shorter than he is …"

As I slowly sank to the ground, I heard Lucilla chirp, "It'll be so romantic!"

THE END

---

to grin like a Cheshire cat – wie ein Honigkuchenpferd grinsen; to emphasize – betonen; knack – *hier:* Händchen

Von Hortense Ullrich u. a.
bei Thienemann erschienen:

Hexen küsst man nicht (1)
Never Kiss a Witch
Liebeskummer lohnt sich (2)
Doppelt geküsst hält besser (3)
Liebe macht blond (4)
Love is Blonde
Wer zuletzt küsst ... (5)
... und wer liebt mich? (6)
Ein Kuss kommt selten allein (7)
Unverhofft liebt oft (8)
Ehrlich küsst am längsten (9)
Andere Länder, andere Küsse (10)
Kein Tanz, kein Kuss (11)
Liebe auf den ersten Blick (12)
Ferien gut, alles gut

Ullrich, Hortense:
And Who Loves Me?
Aus dem Deutschen von David Fermer
ISBN 978 3 522 17881 5

Reihen- und Einbandgestaltung: Birgit Schössow
Innentypografie: Marlis Killermann
Schrift: New Baskerville
Satz: KCS GmbH, Buchholz/Hamburg
Reproduktion: Medienfabrik, Möglingen
Druck und Bindung: Friedrich Pustet, Regensburg

6 5 4 3 2° 08 09 10 11

www.thienemann.de
www.frechemaedchen.de

Hortense Ullrich
Betreff: IrrLäufer
PinkMuffin
BerryBlue
Joachim Friedrich

Hortense Ullrich
Betreff: LiebesWahn
PinkMuffin
BerryBlue
Joachim Friedrich